Men Who Saw Revival

DR. RICK MARTIN
&
DR. ALLEN DOMELLE

© Copyright 2013
Allen Domelle Ministries
ISBN: 978-0-9833193-5-1
All Scripture quotations are from the
King James Bible 1611.
Visit our website at:
oldpathsjournal.com

For more copies:

Allen Domelle Ministries
PO Box 5653
Longview, TX 75608
903.746.9632

TABLE OF CONTENTS

George Whitefield

1714-1770

When the name George Whitefield is mentioned, the image of a man preaching to great crowds in the fields of Great Britain comes to mind. There are some who even consider him the greatest evangelist since the first century. Those who have studied the life of Mr. Whitefield know him to be a man whose heart for souls was as big as the boom in his voice; a man whose Christlike compassion for the lost drove him to preach and consequently reach about one-half million precious souls for Christ.

Born the son of an innkeeper, his father died at an early age. Young George helped his mother work in a tavern. As a mischievous boy, he would attend the church near his home, and then go back to the bar and mimic the pastor to the delight of the drunkards.

While attending Oxford University, he came under the influence of John Wesley and the "Holy Club." Darkness turned to light as George Whitefield experienced the new birth and was forever changed.

He soon became a preacher of the Gospel, and wherever he went he would preach the message, "Ye Must Be Born Again." In his early twenties he preached in the largest churches. He was a man of God who loved people, and they responded in kind. When he told one congregation that he would go to the United States, then a colony of England, the people wept. Seven times in his lifetime he crossed the Atlantic Ocean to preach in the "Colonies" and to help several orphanages he had organized.

Once in America he preached at Harvard University, and it was claimed that every student and professor professed Christ as Saviour! Benjamin Franklin, famous scientist, author and inventor, measured his voice and said it could be distinctly heard from a distance of one-half mile, and that he could be heard at a distance of one mile away if conditions were good. God had given him, it seemed, a supernatural ability in speaking. Benjamin Franklin said, "Whitefield can control and keep hold of a crowd of 30,000 to 40,000 people."

Arriving back in England in 1739, he suddenly found the churches closed to him. Society in England was in a wicked state. It was no shame for statesmen and leaders in society to be publicly drunk. Crime was rampant, in spite of the fact that the death penalty applied to over 160 offenses.

True conversion among the clergy was rare. There were many brilliant and educated clergy. It was fashionable for them to frequent and shine in all public places, except their pulpits. Although many congregations wanted to hear Whitefield preach his message of the new birth, it was repulsive to these ministers.

Nothing could stop George Whitefield from preaching on this basic truth about going to Heaven. It was estimated that he preached on the subject, "Ye Must Be Born Again," over 3,000 times. One critic asked him why he preached so many times on this same subject. He replied, *"Because sir, ye must be, born again!"* This matter is what drove Whitefield – a belief that a person was lost without Christ's forgiveness, and that the new birth was the most important happening in anyone's life.

Having received an invitation, he went to Bristol to preach; however, when he arrived, his invitation had been withdrawn because of his statement that he could produce two cobblers (like vendors) who knew, "more of true Christianity than all the clergy in the city of Bristol."

He said in his diary, *"I had the pleasure of hearing that the mayor and sheriff of Bristol have absolutely forbidden me to preach there any longer because I insisted upon the necessity of the new birth."*

On his way to lunch in Kingswood (about one and a half miles outside the walls of Bristol) on February 17, 1739, he saw the coal miners, who were called "colliers" coming out of the mines. These colliers were wicked and vile men. Even the hardened sailors of that day were afraid of them. Once, upon being cheated out of enjoying the sight of a public hanging of a local criminal, because he had committed suicide rather than being made a public spectacle, they dug up his corpse as revenge for ruining their fun.

These kind of people were completely ignored by the clergy. Although their bodies might befoul the wicked, their souls were immortal. They could only be reached in the open air. Whitefield's good friend, John Wesley, told him that preaching in the open air out in the fields was a "bad notion." Later, upon seeing the results of Whitefield's field preaching, Wesley not only changed his mind, but began preaching in the fields himself.

The miners came up out of the pits, their faces blackened with coal. He felt afraid of what he was about to do, but if the churches were to be closed to him, he should all the more go and preach like Jesus did. Whitefield stood on a small hill, and pitched his voice about 100 yards to a group of colliers walking toward him. He called out, *"Blessed are the poor in spirit, for theirs is the kingdom of Heaven."*

The miners stopped and stared at the person holding a book that they could hear from 100 yards away. His young voice sounded out again, "Matthew, chapter five, and verse three: *'Blessed are the poor in spirit, for theirs is the kingdom of Heaven.'*"

The miners came closer and listened as he told them a story which made them laugh. None had ever heard a preacher tell a joke; most had not even heard a preacher at all. About 200 men gathered as he spoke of Hell as a place being black as their coal pit, and of the certainty of judgment. He talked about Jesus Who was a friend of publicans and sinners, and Who came not to call the righteous, but sinners to repentance. He spoke of the cross and the love of God, and brushed tears from his eyes.

Suddenly, he noticed tears coming from the eyes of a young man on his right. These tears were forming a pale streak on his grimy face. He saw the same thing happen to an old, bent miner on his left, and then more and more of them. He said he saw, *"White gutters made by their tears down their black cheeks."* Whitefield said, *"Blessed be God. I have now broke the ice. I believe I was never more acceptable to my Master than when I was standing beside those hearers in the open field."*

The men invited him to come the next day to speak to their friends and families. About 2,000 people came out to hear him preach. Five days later he preached to 5,000, and two days later to over 10,000. A few days later, he preached at Rosegreen Common to so great a multitude that it covered three acres. The crowd was estimated at 20,000 people.

Whitefield would go to places where a crowd would gather and preach. Public hangings were common, and thousands would gather to witness the event. As soon as the hanging was over, he would climb upon the platform and preach about death and eternal life – with quite an object lesson below. It was often said, "When the body quits twitching, Whitefield starts preaching."

The weather never kept the crowds away. Once, 8,000 came out in the snow, and 12,000 heard him preach during a heavy rain. On another occasion he preached near a horse race, and the 10,000 who had come for the races left to hear him preach.

Once he preached near a carnival where a great crowd was attending. Before long most of the people left the carnival and came to hear the preaching. The owner of the carnival sent out a prize fighter to take care of Whitefield. This brawler had no shirt on. He had a cauliflower ear and a broken nose. Whitefield lifted up his voice and thundered out as loud as he could, *"I am not ashamed of the Gospel of Jesus Christ, for it is the power of God unto salvation."* The prize fighter meekly turned around and went back.

The next day Whitefield came back to preach, so the carnival owner sent a man who threw eggs, parts of dead dogs, and rocks. Whitefield was hit in the mouth with a rotten tomato. Since this didn't stop him, a man climbed a tree next to where he was preaching and dropped his pants. George Whitefield told all the ladies to cover their eyes and he kept on preaching. Not to be deterred, the man urinated on Whitefield, but even that wouldn't stop him. Nothing stopped him. Several times he was hit with stones. One of his evangelist friends was killed by stone throwers during his field preaching.

In the month of May, 1739, he preached to over 500,000 people in the fields. His diary revealed the power of God:

"Sunday, May 6. Preached this morning in Moorfields to about 20,000 people, who were very quiet and attentive, and much affected. Went to public worship morning and evening; and, at six, preached at Kennington. Such a sight I never saw before. I believe there were no less than 50,000 people, and near fourscore coaches, besides great numbers of horses. There was an awful silence among them. God gave me great enlargement of heart. I continued my discourse for an hour and a half, and when I returned home, I was filled with such love, peace, and joy, that I cannot express it. I believe this was partly owing to some opposition I met with yesterday. It is hard for men to kick against the pricks. The more they oppose, the more shall Jesus Christ be exalted. Our adversaries seem to have come to an extremity, while for want of arguments to convince, they are obliged to call out to the civil magistrate to compel me to be silent; but I believe it will be difficult to prove our assemblies in the fields either disorderly or illegal. Friday, June 1. Dined at Old Ford, and gave a short exhortation to a few people in a field, and preached, in the evening, at a place called Mayfair, near Hyde Park Corner. The congregation, I believe, consisted of near 80,000 people. It was, by far, the largest I ever preached to yet. In the time of my prayer, there was a little noise; but they kept a deep silence during my whole discourse. A high and very commodious scaffold was erected for me to stand upon; and though I was weak in myself, yet God strengthened me to speak so loud, that most could hear, and so powerfully, that most, I believe, could feel. All love, all glory be to God through Christ! Sunday, June 3. Preached at Moorfields to a larger congregation than ever. Preached in the evening at Kennington Common, to the most numerous audience I ever yet saw in that place, and collected 34 pounds 5s. When I mentioned my departure from them, they were melted into tears. Fervent prayers

were poured out to God on my behalf, which gave me abundant reason to be thankful to my dear Master."

He preached for one and one-half hours to an estimated 100,000 people at Combusland in Scotland, and over 10,000 people received Christ as Saviour on that day!

He preached hard against sin, and also against the Roman Catholic Church. After visiting a Catholic high mass, he spoke out with his mighty voice to the people: *"There needs to be no other argument against popery than to see their superstition and idolatry in worship."*

George Whitefield gave his all to preaching and teaching, often traveling and preaching three or four times a day. Sometimes he would preach for two hours and preach so hard that his throat would bleed. This schedule finally took a toll on him; but literally to the end of his life, he went on preaching. The following story tells of his last message:

"One day George Whitefield started out to preach in a certain city. On the way, he had to go through some smaller cities. He stopped in one city and the people said, 'Mr. Whitefield, we know you are going to some other city to preach, but please preach for us.' And he preached. He traveled a little further and in another city people who knew him said, 'Please preach for us before you go on to that city.' And he preached. He went through another city. They said, 'Please preach for us.' He stopped several times that day. Finally, late that evening he reached the city where he was supposed to preach, and he preached. He went up to his room and had gone to bed, when he heard people calling his name. He walked over to the window, looked out, and a crowd had gathered. Some of them said, 'Mr. Whitefield, some of us were working today in the fields and we didn't get to hear you preach. Some of the women had to stay at home with the babies and they didn't get to hear

you preach. Now we are here to hear you.' Mr. Whitefield picked up a candle that was on a piece of cardboard, and with his Bible in the other hand, walked out and said, 'I will preach until the light goes out.' Holding that little candle, he did preach until the light went out, then went back into his room and to bed. The next morning they knocked on his door, but there was no answer. They knocked again, but no answer. They knocked harder, but no answer. Then they broke in. Mr. Whitefield was found on his knees beside the bed with a little piece of cardboard with melted wax where the candle had burned out. He literally preached until the light went out."

During that night, or early morning, he had gone on to be with the Lord just after preaching his last sermon. He was only 55 years old.

Will there ever be another George Whitefield? Probably not, but we know that God's power will come upon the thirsty and those who are willing to pay the price as George Whitefield did.

William Carey

1761-1834

William Carey was reared in poverty and became a shoe cobbler in England. As a layman in a Baptist church, he became burdened for the lost in foreign nations after reading a book on the adventures of Captain Cooke. He had a homemade map of the world, and began to pray for the heathen in different areas of the world.

At a meeting of Baptist pastors in 1791, he suggested a topic for the pastors to discuss. The topic centered around the command given to the apostles to go and preach the Gospel to all nations. He asked the pastors if that commandment was not binding on all successive generations including the present one.

An older pastor said, "Young man, sit down! When God pleases to convert the heathen, He'll do it without consulting you and me."

Carey was so troubled by the heartless response that he felt compelled to write a pamphlet on the subject. This pamphlet was used of God to burden others for the cause of sending out foreign missionaries. Soon, a prayer group was started to ask the Almighty to intervene in the hearts of Christians.

The following year, at another meeting of pastors, Carey (now a lay preacher) preached a message where he listed the principles that should guide the foreign missionary movement. It was in this sermon that he challenged the pastors with the statement: "EXPECT GREAT THINGS FROM GOD, ATTEMPT GREAT THINGS FOR GOD."

This time the response was better, and a group of these men began to raise funds for foreign missions; however, there were no missionaries to send. A missionary doctor who had served in India was home. He was trying to raise funds to go back to India, and he wanted a companion to go with him. As they discussed the situation, one of the pastors turned to William Carey and asked, "Are you willing to go to India with him?"

Carey was very willing and prepared to go, but his wife resisted. She told him she would never go since she had three children and was expecting another. Carey took his eight-year-old son Felix, and boarded the ship to go to India without his wife. He wrote his wife a note, *"If I had all the world, I would freely give it to have you and the dear children with me."*

Someone wrote the captain of the ship and said that these men were missionaries. The India Tea Company did not want any missionaries in India and refused to allow them to stay on the ship.

When he returned home, he found his wife now willing to go with him. Realizing now how much she would miss him, she had changed her mind. They found another ship and set sail for India. Arriving in India in 1793, they discovered that this missionary doctor with whom they were traveling had left many debts, and all the money they had entrusted to him had been taken away by creditors. There they were, destitute and stranded in a strange city, and in a foreign land. To make matters worse, his second son died the following year at the age of five.

The work was very slow. Their first convert was baptized seven years later in 1800. Tragedy soon followed after both his wife and missionary partner became mentally ill. The missionary died in 1801; his wife in 1807.

The paganism and cruelty broke his heart, and he set about to do something about two terrible practices. The first was the Hindu practice they carried out at every January festival, of "devoted" mothers throwing their babies into the "sacred" Ganges River. The babies would either drown or be torn apart by crocodiles. Carey's diligent efforts resulted in a new law passed by the government. Soldiers were stationed by the river, and baby sacrifices were stopped.

The other evil practice was called "Sati." Hindus would burn to death the widow of a dead man when he was burned. Although it took 25 years before a law was passed in 1829, Carey's efforts made a lasting effect on this evil.

In spire of great opposition from people in government and from English businessmen, Carey kept on working; "plodding" as he called it. He was never able to go home to England during the 40 years he spent in India, and the road he traveled was paved with tears. Yet, he kept on "plodding." He said late in his life:

"If, after my removal, anyone should think it worth his while to write my life, I will give you a criterion by which you may judge. If he gives me credit for being a plodder, he will describe me justly. Anything beyond this will be too much. I can plod."

Carey's sister wrote of him:

"Whatever he began, he always finished...God's plodder...When he had to work full time to support his family in India – he plodded. When his loving little five year old son died – he plodded. When his wife, depressed by all the tragedy, became insane – he plodded. When she died – he plodded. For 40 years he plodded; giving

the Word of God to the Indians, never looking back nor returning here for a furlough."

Carey just kept on working, winning souls and starting churches. More and more Christians followed his example and left England to preach the Gospel in foreign lands. He started a college to train Christian workers, and the work of God spread across India. His vision and burden to get the Word of God translated into the different Indian dialects was realized as the Scriptures were translated into 34 languages and dialects. When he arrived in India, only two dialects had the Word of God; now almost all of India had access to the Word of God.

On June 9, 1834, William Carey left this world to go to his real Home in Heaven. When he died, he had truly been a man who, "Expected great things from God, and attempted great things for God."

However, it was the Lord Jesus Christ to Whom he pointed men – to His greatness, not his own. (On his deathbed a young Scottish missionary, Alexander Duff came to visit Carey.) They spoke for quite some time until finally William Carey interrupted the young man and said:

"Mr. Duff, you have been speaking about Dr. Carey. Dr. Carey! When I am gone, say nothing about Dr. Carey...speak about Dr. Carey's Saviour."

The greatness, I believe, in the life of William Carey was his great vision of the Gospel being spread to other lands and his part in achieving that. He was the Gospel's man God used to help so many to see that the world is truly every Christian's responsibility. May God give us a world vision so that we too can have a part in the Saviour's command to go into all the world and preach the Gospel.

Adoniram Judson
1788-1850

Adoniram Judson was America's first foreign missionary. On February 19, 1812, he and his new bride Ann left for India. He was a Congregationalist, and having much free time on the ship, he began to study the subject of baptism. Being convinced he was wrong, he became a Baptist by conviction, and soon lost his support. Upon arriving in India, he met William Carey. In spite of Carey's help, the government of India would not allow him to stay and demanded he return to the United States.

Too embarrassed to return, he found a ship going to Burma, a country in which he was much interested. However, he didn't want to go because his wife was expecting their first child. They left in spite of misgivings, and she delivered on the ship, but the baby died. Heartbroken, they arrived in Burma. Ann Judson was so weak that she had to be carried off the ship.

Soon, the Judson's learned what many missionaries find when they arrive in foreign countries – missionary work is very slow. As he began to learn the Burmese language, he passed out tracts and talked to people; but the first year on the field he did not have a single convert. As far as Judson knew, there wasn't a Burmese Christian in Burma. Felix Carey, the son of William Carey, had spent many years in Burma without any visible results.

During his second year there, not a single Burmese was saved through his dedicated efforts. In his third year in Burma, Ann gave birth to their second child; a boy they named Roger. They didn't have any converts, but at least they had a baby boy. Eight months after Roger was born, he became very sick and died. Brokenhearted, the Judson's buried their second child, and still no converts.

Adoniram kept preaching, and finally after six years, on May 5, 1819, a poor riverboat worker named Maung Nau was saved. Two others were also saved, and now he had three baptized converts. That may not seem like much to most Christians, but to Ann and Adoniram Judson, it was like a revival. The Devil began to fight back, and war broke out between England and Burma.

He tried to tell the government officials that he was an American, not an Englishman, but to no avail. All foreigners were imprisoned as spies. In prison, Judson was tortured, and almost starved to death. His wife gave birth to their third child soon after he was imprisoned. They named their daughter Maria.

The war was finally over, and after two years in prison, Judson was freed. His health was so broken that he didn't believe much was going to happen with his life. He felt that if he would just be faithful that other missionaries would follow and see a better harvest, but he was wrong. God was going to bless his faithfulness with a great harvest.

The war had broken down the pride of many, and revival finally came. He began to spend much time traveling away from Ann and Maria. He was at the happiest point in his life because God was doing a work in the hearts of many.

While traveling, he received a letter from his wife that Maria was very sick. Soon after that word, he received a dreaded black sealed envelope signifying someone had died. He grieved as he thought of poor Maria, and wondered if he would ever have a child grow to adulthood.

As he opened the letter and began to read, he simply couldn't believe the message it contained. The third sentence read, "To sum up the unhappy tidings in a few words – Mrs. Judson is no more."

All at once, he was overwhelmed with the weight of what had happened. He began to weep, softly at first, then with great sobbing, Finally, as the meaning of the letter was fully realized, he leaned forward on his writing table and put his head on his arms, wondering how he could ever stay in Burma without Ann.

He went home and picked up his little girl, who was all he had left as family. Little did he realize that exactly six months after he buried his wife, little Maria would be buried next to her under a hopia tree outside their home.

Still, Adoniram Judson stayed in Burma because he loved the Burmese people, and because he loved the Lord. He had begun translating the Bible into the Burmese language before he was imprisoned. After 18 years his work was completed.

Adoniram Judson's life seemed to have one tragedy after another. His second wife also died in Burma. Through it all, God molded this man into a man of God who reached Burma with the Gospel.

Adoniram Judson died on a ship that was going back to the United States. He had only been home one time in 39 years. He was buried at sea in the Indian Ocean.

Several years after he died, the government of Burma did a survey. Officials estimated that there were at least 210,000 Christians – and these were Christians who would readily admit they were Christians, as they would be persecuted for saying so. One out of 58 people in

Burma were not only saved, but willing to testify to their salvation, primarily due to the life of Adoniram Judson. It can truly be said of this man, "He saw revival."

He was a man who cared little for self. He would say, *"First or last, honored or unknown, what does it matter in God's sight? I must do His will, whatever the cost."*

Charles Finney
1791-1875

Probably no name is more recognized when the subject of revival is mentioned than is the name of Charles Finney.

As a young attorney, Charles Finney found many references to the Bible in his law books. He decided to buy a Bible, and was soon spending much of his time studying the Scriptures, and as a result he became concerned for his soul. However, pride became an obstacle to his accepting Christ. He was unwilling to let anyone know that he was studying the Bible. If anyone would come in, he would throw the law books on top of the Bible to hide what he was doing.

On October 10, 1821, at the age of 21, he decided he would settle these questions of his salvation and make his peace with God. Great joy filled his heart when he got saved. He said:

"No words can express the wonderful love that was shed abroad in my heart. I wept aloud with joy and love; and...I bellowed out the unutterable gushing of my heart. These waves came over me and over me and over me one after another until I recollect I cried out, 'I shall die if these waves continue to pass over me, Lord, I cannot bear any more.'"

That same evening a choir member of a church he had attended came to his office and saw him weeping. He asked, "Mr. Finney, what ails you? Are you in pain?"

"No, but so happy I cannot live," he replied. The church member rushed out of the office and found a leader in that choir to come and hear his testimony. At the conclusion of Finney's conversion testimony, this man fell to the floor and cried, "Do pray for me to be converted."

Upon seeing several others saved soon after this experience, Finney had the impression that God wanted him to preach the Gospel and that he must begin immediately.

"I found that I was unwilling to do anything else. I had no longer any desire to practice law...I had no disposition to make money. I had no hungering and thirsting after worldly pleasures and amusements in any direction...Nothing, it seemed, could be put in competition with the worth of souls; and no labor...could be so sweet...as that of holding up Christ to a dying world."

When Finney began to preach, American churches were in a bad condition, being divided basically into two groups, the Universalists and the Hyper-Calvinists. The doctrine of election was preached by the Hyper-Calvinists so that Christians as individuals and churches felt no responsibility to spread the Gospel.

Finney preached that Christ died for all men, and that it was the responsibility of every believer to spread the Gospel. This preaching stirred up much opposition, but also a conviction never experienced before set into some Christians and revival began.

He was given the responsibility to preach in two small villages in New York. At one of these villages, Evans Mills, he would not only preach on Sundays, but also weeknights. The people enjoyed his sermons, but when he concluded that they had never experienced the new birth, and that they would not make a decision to accept

Christ, he gave them an ultimatum one evening in his message:

"Now I must know your minds, and I want all of you who will give your pledge to make your peace with God immediately, to rise up; but all of you who are resolved not to become Christians, and wish me to understand so, and Christ to understand so, remain sitting."

This statement shocked the congregation!

"They looked at one another and at me, and all sat still, just as I expected." He spoke again, *"Then you are committed. You have taken your stand. You have rejected Christ and His Gospel...You may remember as long as you live that you have thus publicly committed yourselves against the Saviour."*

The congregation left, some angry, some with heads hung down in shame. One of the few members, a deacon, who was truly born again, came to him and said, "Brother Finney, you've got them. They cannot rest under this, and you will see the results."

Together they spent the next day in prayer and fasting, something Finney always practiced when results did not come. By the next evening they felt assured the power of God would be revealed. The church was packed as he preached. He said when he preached the conviction was so strong it was like a hammer breaking a rock. Instead of giving an invitation, he dismissed the service. It was more than the people could bear, and that night many were heard crying out to God, and many were saved.

Early in his ministry he met a preacher named Daniel Nash. This man was a great man of prayer, and he joined Finney. As Finney would preach, Nash would go to a nearby house and pray. The results were a work of the Holy Spirit in the lives of those listening to Finney.

Everywhere Finney went revival followed. Estimates of those saved through his preaching range from 100,000 to as many as 500,000.

He was accused of letting down the dignity of the pulpit, and criticized for not preaching like the other ministers did. He answered, *"Show me the fruits of your ministry, and if they so far exceed mine as to give me evidence that you have found a more excellent way, I will adopt your views."*

It did not matter how wicked the place was, Finney would go and preach, and revival would follow. He had heard about a wicked village and decided to go there and preach. He preached on the story of Sodom and Gomorrah and selected the text, *"Up, get you out of this place; for the Lord will destroy the city."*

He didn't realize the place was called "Sodom," and the only good man in the village was named "Lot." Finney said:

"The people looked as if they were angry. They looked at each other and at me. Their anger rose higher and higher as I continued...The congregation began to fall from their seats and cried for mercy. If I had a sword in each hand, I could not have cut them off their seats as fast as they fell. Indeed, nearly the whole congregation were either on their knees or prostrate. In less than two minutes, everyone prayed for himself, who was able to speak at all."

The son and grandson of the man named Lot both were converted at that meeting, and both became preachers. The grandson enrolled in Finney's Bible school.

He went to DeKalb and had many Presbyterians and Methodists saved, Finney recalled later:

"A Roman Catholic priest who came from Ogdensburg to be measured for a suit of clothes was converted on the spot, and this spread the revival in all directions."

After a few services Finney had no chance to preach, for everywhere people were seeking the Lord. A friend of Finney's said, "Finney could only sit still and see the salvation of the Lord, by the spontaneous movement of the Holy Ghost in convicting and converting sinners."

Finney said the most amazing display of God's power in his life came one day as he went to visit a cotton factory at New York Mills, a small town near Utica, New York. Prior to his visit to the factory, more than 500 converts were reported in the short time he had been in Utica.

Unusual conversions were reported. A proud, disbelieving school teacher came to make light of what was happening to her friends who had been saved, when she too was suddenly convicted of her lost condition. Not long afterward, she married a Mr. Guilick, who became a missionary to the Sandwich Islands, where God used them both mightily.

Everyone in the area heard what was going on, and the people were divided. A great number of those against the meeting were openly opposing it. As Finney walked into the cotton mill, one of the opponents of the meeting, a young lady employee, saw him. Looking at her co-employee, she began to laugh. Some writers say she made a cynical remark about Finney and his meeting. In a spirit of prayer, Charles Finney simply looked at this young lady without saying a word. As he kept looking at her, being grieved by her criticism, the lady stopped working as she had broken her thread. She became so upset that she couldn't repair the thread and start again. The Spirit of God mightily convicted her of her sin to the point that she began to weep. Soon her companions were convicted and began to weep. A chain reaction occurred as hundreds began to be overcome by their lost condition.

The factory owner, seeing this, was deeply moved himself and said, "Stop the mill, and let the people attend to religion, for it is far more important that our souls be saved than the factory run."

All the workers were assembled in a very large room, and Finney said, *"A more powerful meeting I scarcely ever attended."* Within a few days nearly every employee was saved (some accounts say all were saved). Several authors say there were 3,000 employees in this factory.

Others say the greatest outpouring of the Holy Spirit's power was in the revival held in Rochester, New York. In 1830, over 10,000 people were converted in that city; almost the whole city. The only theatre in town was converted into a livery stable, the circus into a soap and candle factory, and the rum shops (bars) were closed.

Before he arrived in Rochester, wickedness abounded and dance halls flourished. One of the first conversions was the wife of a prominent lawyer who previously had been a worldly woman. She was afraid that Finney's meetings would interfere with the pleasures and amusements she had. Instead, she got saved. Several days afterward Finney did something he had never done before. He gave a call for all in the service who were willing, to come forward and be prayed for and dealt with concerning salvation. Finney said:

"It was soon seen that the Lord was aiming at the highest classes of society. The lawyers, physicians, merchants, and indeed all the most intelligent people became interested and more easily influenced...a large number of lawyers, nearly all the judges, bankers, merchants and master mechanics and leading men and women in the city were converted."

Revival, which started with the poor and common people, as it always has, spread to the influential in society, and the Lord Jesus welcomed them all into His Kingdom.

The spirit of prayer and crowds were so great that people, although greatly wanting to attend, volunteered to stay away from the overcrowded services to pray for the lost.

A pastor and an opponent of Finney's revival at Rochester, Dr. Lyman Beecher, soon changed his opinion and became a firm backer and believer. He said it was his opinion that, this revival was, *"...the greatest work of God, and the greatest revival of religion the world has ever seen in so short a time."*

Edwin Beecher, Dr. Beecher's son, was a pastor in Boston, Massachusetts. When Finney came to preach in his church he said:

"He preached to a crowded house; the most powerful sermon I ever heard...no one can form any conception of the power of this appeal. It rings in my ears ever to this day."

To Finney, revival was something that would come anywhere where certain conditions were met. He said:

"A revival can be expected when Christians have a spirit of prayer for revival."

"A revival is no more a revival than a crop of wheat. In any community revival can be secured from Heaven when heroic souls enter the conflict determined to win or die, or if need be, win and die."

"Revival is a renewed conviction of sin and repentance, followed by an intense desire to live in obedience to God. It is giving up one's will to God in deep humility."

The same Holy Spirit power in the life of Charles Finney is available to you and me as the Word of God says, *"I will pour water upon him that is thirsty and floods upon the dry ground; I will pour out my Spirit upon thy seed, and my blessing upon their offspring."* (Isaiah 44:3)

Dwight L. Moody
1837-1899

Born February 5, 1837, Dwight L. Moody grew up in a home without a father. His father passed away when Dwight was only four years old. Some neighbors told his mother that it would be impossible to rear seven boys and that they would probably end up in jail. When Moody preached her funeral years later, he reminded his hometown friends, *"If everyone had a mother like my mother, there would be no need for jails."*

Mrs. Moody was always cheerful, but cried herself to sleep every night for the first year after her husband died. Her sorrow drove her to rear her boys for God. When her husband died, the creditors took everything they could find, including their firewood! Although destitute, Mrs. Moody had a heart of gold and often shared what little food they had with beggars. Little Dwight never forgot the compassion his mother shared for the poor and unloved.

The boys were so poor that they were taught to carry their shoes and socks to church to save them from wear. Although unsaved, Dwight recruited other children to go with him.

At the age of 17, he could hardly read or write. He moved to Boston, Massachusetts. His life's goal was to make $100,000 and become rich. After landing a job selling shoes, he found a Sunday school to attend. The teacher, Edward Kimball, gave him a Bible and began to pray for Moody's salvation.

Although very nervous, Mr. Kimball went to visit Moody at the shoe store where he worked. After getting up enough courage, he entered the store and began to share the plan of salvation with Moody. That day was the beginning of a revival that covered two continents and had a harvest of over 1 million souls. Since that day, soul winners have been challenged to never underestimate the value of a single soul-winning opportunity. The person they win may become another D.L. Moody.

Moody recalls later how his life was changed:

"Before my conversion I worked to be saved, now I work because I am saved. I remember the first morning after I trusted Christ. I think the sun shone a great deal brighter than it had before, and as I walked in Boston Common and heard the birds singing in the tree, I thought that they were all singing a song to me."

Moving to Chicago at the age of 19, he began attending church. In that time, it was common for churches to charge people who attended their church by the bench or pew. Soon, Moody had so many visitors attending the services that he had to rent four pews. His business had him traveling around Chicago, and the condition of the children in the slums began to convict him to do something. Joining another Sunday school, he applied as a teacher, but was told there were no openings. He volunteered to recruit his own pupils and rounded up 18 dirty, poor children off the streets.

Two years later in 1858, he started his own Sunday school in a vacant bar. The mayor of Chicago, upon hearing of his plans, and understanding the problems the city faced with these children, let him use a large building free of charge. He brought some of the children on horse-drawn carts to church.

In Moody's Sunday school, the children could attend any class they wanted, so the best teachers would have the most children.

Moody tried to help these children from off the streets who knew little but poverty, fighting, and ignorance. He gave some of the older children responsibilities such as keeping order in the Sunday school. These were known as "Moody's bodyguards."

Needless to say, "Moody's bodyguards" had a few "rough edges" in carrying out this responsibility. One day a new boy came to Sunday school and took his seat with his cap still on. Moody tried to teach the children that this was not mannerly. Upon seeing this transgression, one of the "bodyguards" walked up to him, and without warning planted a stunning blow between the eyes that sent him to the floor. "I'll teach you not to enter Moody's Sunday school with your hat on!" he told the stunned visitor. Well, these bodyguards had a little to learn concerning proper manners, too! But, they did know something about loyalty, and the Lord began to change their lives.

One "scholar," as they called their students, moved to another part of the city. He continued to come to Sunday school from this long distance even though it required several hours of walking, often through snow. Someone asked him why he went so far when there were other Sunday schools closer to his home. He replied, "They may be good for others, but not for me, because they love a fellow over there."

When students would miss Sunday School for several weeks, Moody would go get them. He was nicknamed, "Crazy Moody" because of the great lengths he would go to get children to return to his Sunday school. During this time D.L. Moody became a personal soul winner. Up to this time, he was bringing children to Sunday school, but not winning souls out in the streets and homes.

God opened his eyes through a certain event. Moody tells in his own words what happened.

"There was a class of young ladies in the school who were without exception the most frivolous set I've ever met. One Sunday the teacher was ill, and I took that class. They laughed in my face, and I felt like opening the door and telling them all to get out and never come back. That week the teacher of the class came into the store where I worked. He was pale and looked very ill.

What is the trouble?' I asked. 'I have had another hemorrhage of my lungs.' he answered. 'The doctor says I cannot live on Lake Michigan, so I am going to New York State. I suppose I am going home to die.' He seemed greatly troubled, and when I asked him why he replied, 'Well, I have never led any of my class to Christ. I really believe I have done the girls more harm than good.' I had never heard anyone talk like that before, and it set me thinking. After a while I said, 'Suppose you go and tell them how you feel. I will go with you in a carriage, if you want to go…'

He consented, and we started out together. It was one of the best journeys I ever had on Earth. We went to the house of one of the girls, and the teacher talked to her about her soul. There was no laughing then. Tears stood in her eyes before long. After he had explained the way of life, he suggested that we have prayer. He asked me to pray. True, I had never done such a thing as to pray to God to convert a young lady there and then. But, we prayed, and God answered our prayer. We went to other houses. He would go upstairs, and be all out of breath, and he would tell the girls what he had come for. It wasn't long before they broke down and sought salvation.

When his strength gave out, I took him to his lodgings. The next day we went out again. At the end of 10 days he came to the store with his face literally shining. 'Mr. Moody' he said, 'the last one of my class has yielded herself to Christ!' I tell you, we had a time of rejoicing!

He had to leave the next night, so I called the class together that night for a prayer meeting, and there God kindled a fire in my soul that has never gone out. The height of my ambition had been to be a successful merchant. If I had known that meeting was going to take that ambition out of me, I might not have gone. But, how many times I have thanked God since for that meeting.

The dying teacher sat in the midst of his class, and talked with them, and read the 14th chapter of John. We tried to sing, 'Blest Be the Tie That Binds,' after which we knelt to pray. I was just rising from my knees, when one of the class began to pray for her dying teacher. Another prayed, and another, and before we rose the whole class had prayed. As I went out I said to myself, 'Oh God, let me die rather than lose the blessing I have received tonight!'

The next evening I went to the depot to say goodbye to that teacher. Just before the train started, one of the class members came. Before long, without any prearrangement, they were all there. What a meeting that was! We tried to sing, but we broke down. The last we saw of that dying teacher he was standing on the platform of the rear car, his finger pointing upward, telling us to meet him in Heaven!"

At this point of Moody's life (the age of 23), he decided to give up his business. He had done well, but decided to live off his savings and serve the Lord full-time. As he put it, *"I had become disqualified for business; it has become distasteful to me. I had got a taste of another world, and cared no more for making money."*

His Sunday school developed into the largest church in Chicago, as it was not long before the parents began to come. Interest was so great that the church not only met on Sunday, but had services almost every night of the week.

Humanly speaking, Moody seemed to be unprepared to lead this work. He felt uneducated, and his first attempts at speaking were awkward. Little by little, he overcame these obstacles. Both opposition and critics tried to stop Moody. One critic, a member of the church Moody first attended in Chicago, told him that his zeal for God was wonderful, but warned him not to preach until his grammar improved. "You make too many mistakes in grammar," he told Moody.

Moody humbly responded, *"I know I make mistakes, but I'm doing the best I can with what I've got."* Then he looked at his critic straight in the eye. *"Look here, friend, you've got grammar enough. What are you doing with it for the Master?"*

Moody's success in his Sunday school resulted in invitations to come and speak about it. In addition, people came from long distances to learn the methods he used to organize his Sunday school.

In 1867, Moody decided to visit Great Britain to study their methods of Christian work. He was particularly interested to hear Charles Hadden Spurgeon preach, and to meet George Mueller, who had built several large orphanages near Bristol.

While visiting Dublin, Ireland, he met Mr. Henry Varley, a well-known evangelist. As they sat on a seat in a public park, Mr. Varley said, *"The world has yet to see what God will do with, and for, and through, and in and by the man who is fully consecrated to Him."*

This statement greatly challenged the heart of D.L. Moody. Moody thought, *"He said, 'A man.' He did not say, 'A great man,' nor 'A learned man,' nor 'A smart man,' simply 'A man.' I will try my utmost to be that man."*

In England, he also met a preacher named Henry Morehouse, who was known as "the boy preacher" because of his boyish looks. Morehouse asked if he could preach at his church when he visited Chicago. He did preach at Moody's church for seven nights, and each message about the love of God was from John 3:16. Up until then, Moody said he would preach that, *"...God was behind the sinner with a double-edged sword, ready to hew him down...I preach now that God is behind the sinner with love."*

From that time on, D.L. Moody preached with tears! Dr. R.W. Dale, a leading "non-conformist" in England remarked that Moody had a right to preach the Gospel to so many people *"...because he could never speak to a lost person without tears of Christian compassion in his eyes."*

In 1871, something else happened that multiplied the usefulness of his life. Two ladies in his church would tell him after church on Sundays that they were praying for him. He said, *"Why don't you pray for the people instead?"* The ladies replied, *"Because you need the filling of the Holy Spirit."*

He exclaimed, *"I need power? I thought I had the power!"* He reminded them that he had the largest church in Chicago, and that there had been many conversions.

However, it was not long before God began to deal with him concerning this matter. Soon after the great Chicago fire occurred, and Moody's church building was burnt to the ground, he went to New York City to raise funds for the reconstruction of his church, but more than his desire to rebuild was the thirst he had for God's power. He explained what happened while in New York City.

"I was crying all the time that God would fill me with His Spirit. Well, one day, in the city of New York – oh, what a day! I cannot describe it, I seldom refer to it; it is almost too sacred an experience to name. Paul had an experience of which he never spoke for fourteen years. I can only say that God revealed Himself to me, and I had such an experience of His love that I had to ask Him to stay His hand. I went to preaching again. The sermons were not different; I did not present any new truths; and yet, hundreds were converted. I would not now be placed back where I was before that blessed experience if you should give me all the world – it would be as the small dust of the balance."

God began to use D.L. Moody in revival campaigns in Great Britain. In York, the meeting lasted five weeks, and meeting places were normally full long before services began. A multitude of souls were saved.

In Glasgow, Scotland, at the closing service at the Crystal Palace, the building was so packed with people that Moody could not enter. A crowd of 20,000 to 30,000 were outside who also could not enter. Moody decided to preach on top of a cab to them. In Edinburg, he spoke to as many as 30,000 persons at one time. He held meetings in Great Britain from 1873 to 1875, and England saw revival unlike anything it had seen since the days of George Whitefield and Charles Wesley.

In Liverpool, over 14,000 children attended his children's meeting. Moody said later, *"If I had my life to live over, I would give all my time to children."* Moody realized that when God saves an adult, He saves a soul; but when He saves a child, He saves a life as well – a life time that can be dedicated in the Master's service.

London was a wicked city when D.L. Moody arrived for a campaign. There were 117,000 habitual criminals on the police register, and it was growing at a rate of 30,000 a year. They had 38,000 drunkards appear annually before its magistrates. It was said, *"It's many beer shops and gin palaces would, if placed side by side, stretch from Charing Cross to Portsmouth, a distance of 73 miles."*

For four months Moody labored in London. He set up six different meeting places and preached an average of twice a day. The 285 services Moody preached were attended by 2,530,000. For 120 days he spoke to an average of 21,000 people a day, an amazing feat without the help of a microphone! Revival among the Christians and the lost in London took place. One pastor remarked of the London meeting, *"Such a movement the world has not seen since the days of Whitefield and Wesley. He has proved the power of elementary truths over the hearts of men more mightily than all the learned profession and eloquent pastors of England could do."*

It was on this trip that seven young students at Cambridge University, later to be known as the "Cambridge Seven," surrendered to go to China as foreign missionaries. C.T. Studd was one of those students.

Upon arriving in the United States, Moody and Ira Sankey, his song leader, held great meetings in Brooklyn, Chicago, Philadelphia, Boston, New York, and many other cities, always relying on the power of the Holy Spirit for the salvation of souls and revival among Christians. He spent much time building up two Bible schools he had started – one in Chicago, and one in Northfield, Massachusetts.

Moody continued preaching until he died in 1899 at the age of 62. He was so ill, he couldn't walk after his last meeting in Kansas City. Once they brought him to the pulpit, he was able to speak for over one hour to the 15,000 people in attendance. His last sermon was on "Excuses," and a great number of souls were saved.

He returned to Northfield, Massachusetts and died one month later. On his deathbed this account is given:

"...about 6:00 am he quieted down, and soon fell into a natural sleep. He awoke in about an hour. He was heard speaking in slow and measured words, saying, 'Earth receded; Heaven opens before me.' His son's first impulse was to try to arouse him from what he thought was a dream. 'No, this is no dream, Will,' he said. 'It is beautiful! It is like a trance! If this is death, it is sweet! There is no valley here! God is calling me, and I must go!' Turning to his wife, he said, 'Mama, you have been a good wife to me.' With this he became unconscious."

It was said of D.L. Moody that he never preached without tears. Once someone criticized him after hearing him cry during his message. He walked up to Moody and said, *"Mr. Moody, it is unfair for you to cry during your sermon. For, after all, you are only cheating people into Heaven."* Moody replied, *"Sir, my prayer to God is that I can cheat a million souls into Heaven before I die."*

God did use D.L. Moody to reach a million souls. God used him because D.L. Moody cared, and because he cared, he could not preach to lost men without great compassion and tears. The Holy Spirit filled D.L. Moody, and the same Holy Spirit power Moody had is still available today.

Hudson Taylor
1832-1905

Before Hudson Taylor was born, even his evangelist father (James Taylor) dedicated him to the people of China. He had become very concerned about the Chinese after reading a book on the travels of Captain Basil Hall. James was led to pray that if God were to give him a son, he would give that son back to God to go to China to preach the Gospel. However, Hudson Taylor never knew of this promise until seven years after he had sailed to China in 1854.

The health of young Hudson was so bad, that all hope was given up for him to go to China. At the age of 15, he dedicated himself wholly to God to use him as He pleased. A pastor loaned him a book called. *"Medhurst's China."* When the pastor asked him why he wanted it, Hudson told the man of God that God had called him to spend his life as a missionary in China.

He began to serve the Lord by teaching Sunday school, passing out tracts, and visiting the poor and sick. Believing a knowledge of medicine would help him in China, he became a medical assistant to a doctor. Although his salary was very small, he decided to live on one third of his salary and to give God the other two thirds. He lived on rice and oatmeal...

"In this way I had more than two thirds of my income available for other purposes, and my experience was that the less I spent on myself and the more I gave away, the fuller of happiness and blessing did my soul become."

Soon after arriving in China in 1854 at the age of 22, it was apparent to Hudson Taylor that all the missionaries were staying near the coastal cities, and the inland parts of China were not being penetrated with the Gospel.

While studying hard at learning two dialects, he made trips into the interior. Although there were many robbers, and foreigners were warned not to go, Taylor traveled there often and found the people were very friendly.

To reach the Chinese, he humbled himself and shaved his head and began to dress like the Chinese. The other missionaries ridiculed him. Determined, he set out again, going village to village, preaching and passing out tracts. From May 8 to June 1, 1855, he preached in 58 cities, towns and villages. Foreigners who risked traveling to places like Hudson did without the proper papers could be tortured, or even put to death as a spy.

It wasn't long before he found a like-minded missionary. William Burns also had a burden to reach into inland China. Like Taylor he lived simply, believing that a Christian should have few wants. He also had a sense of humor as well. The two men began preaching in Southern Kiangso and North Chekiang.

Although Taylor was younger, when Burns saw the open doors that came to Taylor by wearing Chinese dress, Bums too began to do the same. William Burns had a lasting influence on Taylor, especially his strong belief that evangelization was the great work of the church – a view only a few had in that day.

Many trials and unusual experiences happened to him during these years. When England bombarded Canton in 1857, news spread to Ningpo where he lived. A plot was made to kill him and the other foreigners in that city. About a month later, 50 to 60 Portuguese missionaries were massacred in broad daylight. God intervened in Hudson Taylor's behalf, and his life was spared.

A great burden to Hudson Taylor was the fact that the Mission Society that supported him had many debts in China. He said,

"Personally I had always avoided debt, and kept within my salary, though at times only by very careful economy...but the society itself was in debt. The quarterly bills which I and the others were instructed to draw were often met by borrowed money, and a correspondence commenced which terminated in the following year by my resigning from conscientious motives. To me it seemed that the teaching of God's Word was unmistakably clear: 'Owe no man anything.'"

Resigning was a hard decision, as then he would have no support. It was especially difficult because he met a young missionary lady and desired to marry her as soon as possible.

Two years later in 1860, he became very ill and returned to England to regain his health. In England God began to open doors to get across his burden for inland China. His home pastor, who was also the editor of the *Baptist Magazine*, requested that he write a series of articles about China. These articles caused some interest in inland China. At this point in his life, Hudson Taylor became deeply burdened to pray for many new missionaries to go to China. In these magazine articles, he gave facts, such as, one of every four people in the world lived in China. He wrote that the number of missionaries had not grown, but had actually decreased to only 90, down from 118 the previous winter.

His burden was overwhelming:

"Meanwhile a million a month were dying in that land, dying without God. It was burned into my very soul. For two or three months the conflict was intense. I scarcely slept night or day more than an hour at a time, and feared I should lose my reason. Yet, I did not give in. To no one could I speak freely, not even to my wife. She saw, doubtless, that something was going on; but I felt I must refrain as much as possible from laying upon her a burden so crushing – these souls."

At Perth, Scotland, at a conference for Christian leaders, Hudson Taylor was allowed to speak about China, although most of these leaders were apathetic to the great need of evangelizing foreign nations. God used Hudson Taylor to bring a great conviction upon the hearts and the minds of these Christian leaders. This meeting marked the beginning of a large effort to evangelize inland China. At this meeting he told the story of how one day, near the city of Sungkiang, he and a Chinese passenger were preparing to come ashore from a boat. When he looked around, he noticed the passenger had disappeared. He heard a splash and thought the man must have fallen in the water. The boatman told man told him in a very unconcerned manner, "Yes, it was over there he went down." Feeling helpless, he told how he found a fisherman with a dragnet – just what he needed.

"Come and drag over this spot. A man is drowning!"
"Veh din,' was the amazing reply." (Veh din meaning, "It is not convenient")
"Don't talk of convenience! Quickly come, or it will be too late."
"We are busy fishing."
"Never mind your fishing! Come – only come at once! I will pay you well."

"How much will you give us?"

"Five dollars! – only don't stand talking. Save life without delay!"

"Too little," they shouted across the water. *"We will not come for less than thirty dollars."*

"But I have not so much with me. I will give you all I've got."

"And, how much may that be?"

"Oh, I don't know. About fourteen dollars."

Finally they came, and the first time they passed the net through the water, they brought up the missing man; but it was too late. His death was most certainly the result of their indifference. Indignation and rage swept through the audience as they could hardly believe anyone could be so heartless. But, a terrible sense of guilt came over the audience as he continued his message:

"Is the body, then, of so much more value than the soul? We condemn those heathen fishermen. We say they were guilty of the man's death – because they could easily have saved him, and did not do it. But, what of the millions whom we leave to perish, and that eternally? What of the plain command, 'Go ye into all the world and preach the Gospel to every creature…'"

He went on to say that in Scotland, with a population of 4 million, several thousand ministers were needed, an average of one pastor for every 2,000 people. In China, there was not even one missionary for every 4 million souls. What if Scotland had only one preacher with its 4 million souls? He preached on:

"Do you believe that each unit of these millions has an immortal soul, and that there is 'none other name under heaven given among men' save the precious name of Jesus 'whereby we we must be saved?' Do you believe

that He and He alone is 'the way, the truth, and the life' and that no man cometh unto the Father but by Him? If so, think of the condition of these unsaved souls and examine yourself in the sight of God to see whether you are doing your utmost to make Him known to them or not. It will not do to say that you have no special call to go to China. With these facts before you, you need rather to ascertain whether you have a special call to stay at home. If in the sight of God you cannot say you are sure that you have a special call to stay at home, why are you disobeying the Saviour's plain command to go?"

The conviction ran so deep that the meeting broke up in silence. Soon after this, Hudson Taylor started the China Inland Mission. He describes what kind of missionary they were looking for:

"While thankful for any educational advantages that candidates may have enjoyed, we attach far greater importance to spiritual qualifications. We desire men who believe that there is a God, and that He is both intelligent and faithful, and who therefore trust Him; who believe that He is the Rewarder of those who diligently seek Him, and are therefore men of prayer. We desire men who believe the Bible to be the Word of God, and who, accepting the declaration 'All power is given unto me' are prepared therefore, to go to the remotest parts of the interior of China, expecting to find His arm a sufficient strength and stay. We desire men who believe in eternity and live for it... We do not send men to China as our agents. But men who believe that God has called them to work, who go there to labour for God, and can therefore trust Him...to supply their temporal needs, we gladly cooperate with – providing, if needful, outfit and passage money, and such measure of support as circumstances call for and we are able to supply. Our faith is sometimes tried, but God

always proves Himself faithful, and at the right time and in the right way supplies all our need. The only men who will be happy with us, are those who have this world under their feet: and I do venture to say, that such men will find a happiness they never dreamed of or thought possible down here...If, after prayerfully considering the matter, you still feel drawn to engage in such work, I shall be only too glad to hear from you again."

His friend and supporter of many years, Mr. W.T. Berger, worked with Hudson Taylor, representing him in Great Britain, while Hudson Taylor went back to China with 24 missionaries; each one came to China by faith.

Upon arriving in China in 1865, he found that some of his new recruits were not prepared to take on the Chinese dress and live by the principles they had claimed to believe. Some complained about living conditions, which were better than Hudson Taylor's were when he first arrived in China. An older missionary from another missionary society became jealous of Taylor and began to sow the seeds of discontent among the missionaries. Several wrote to Mr. Berger exaggerating the difficulties they faced and criticized Taylor, asking that he be removed.

Taking the course of true friendship, Mr. Berger wrote to Taylor, sent him the letters, and said, "...be sure, my dear Brother, whatever Mr.___ may have penned, you hold the same place in our hearts as before."

In spite of this heartache of seeing the attitude of these new missionaries, Taylor never became bitter. He wrote back to Mr. Berger:

"That you may be enabled to cast upon God the terrible trial resulting from Mr.___'s conduct, and from those acting with him, I earnestly pray. Let us not fear, dear

Brother, anything but our own failings...I quite expect God will appear for us in the right time...The Lord will bring all these things to a calm in due time, I quite think."

If this were not enough, it seemed God would allow one more trial to come. In 1867, he wrote to Mr. Berger again, this time expressing his concerns about his little eight-year-old daughter, Gracie:

"Beloved Brother, I know not how to write or how to refrain. I seem to be writing, almost, from the inner chamber of the King of kings. Surely this is holy ground. I am trying to pen a few lines by the couch on which my darling little Gracie lies dying. Her complaint is hydrocephalus. Dear Brother, our flesh and our heart fail, but God is the strength of our heart and our portion forever. It was no vain nor unintelligent act when, knowing this land, its people and its climate, I laid my wife and children, with myself, on the altar for this service. And He whom so unworthily, with much of weakness and failure, yet in simplicity and godly sincerity, we are and have been seeking to serve, and not without some measure of success – has not left us now."

He makes no mistakes; but the loss was overwhelming:

"Our dear little Gracie! How we miss her! As I take the walks I used to take with her tripping at my side, the thought comes anew like a throb of agony. Is it possible that I shall never more feel the pressure of that little hand, never more hear the sweet prattle of those dear lips, never more see the spark of those bright eyes? And yet, she is not lost. I would not have her back again. She is far holier, far happier than she could ever have been here."

Through it all, he never complained. He once said, *"It is not the greatness of our troubles as the littleness of our spirit which makes us complain."*

Three years later, on July 7, 1870, his wife Maria gave birth to a son. An attack of cholera took the baby's life 13 days later. Three days after their son was buried, Hudson Taylor faced his greatest trial of all, the loss of his dear wife.

I've read the lives of a number of great missionary wives, but none exceeded the godliness of Maria Taylor. I've not read of one who encouraged her husband more. He shares his last moments with her:

"By the time it was dawn, the sunlight revealed the deathlike hue of her countenance. Even my love could no longer deny, not her danger, but that she was actually dying. As soon as I was sufficiently composed, I said:

'My darling, do you know that you are dying?'

'Dying!' she replied. 'Do you think so? What makes you think so?'

I said, 'I can see it, Darling. Your strength is giving way.'

'Can it be so? I feel no pain, only weariness.'

'Yes, you are going Home. You will soon be with Jesus.'

My precious wife thought of my being left alone at a time of so much trial, with no companion like herself, with whom I had been wont to bring every difficulty to the Throne of Grace. 'I am so sorry,' she said, and paused as if half correcting herself for the feeling. 'You are not sorry to go to be with Jesus?' Never shall I forget the look with which she answered, 'Oh, no! It is not that. You know, Darling, that for ten years past there has not been a cloud between me and my Saviour. I cannot be sorry to go to

Him; but it does grieve me to leave you alone at such a time. Yet...He will be with you and meet all your need'"

For 35 years after he buried his wife and two children, Hudson Taylor gave his life to the Chinese people. God blessed him because he always tried to follow the Lord. He once said, *"God gives His best for those who leave the choice with Him."*

He prayed and trusted God to send a great number of workers for inland China. He believed that you just never trust the Lord too much. His challenge was this: *"We have heard of many people who trusted God too little, but have you ever heard of anyone who trusted Him too much?"*

The China Inland Mission grew to over 1,300 missionaries. Many churches were started, and probably more souls were saved as a result of the life of Hudson Taylor than any other missionary.

He was not the only hero of the China Inland Mission as at least 108 missionaries (including 21 of their children) were murdered in different conflicts.

No one loved China like Hudson Taylor. He told a friend one day, *"If I had a thousand lives to give, China would claim every single one of them."*

Although few men ever saw the results of revival like Hudson Taylor, he is not remembered most for revivals; rather, he is to be remembered for his Christ-likeness. Arthur Glasser says it best in his book, *J. Hudson Taylor – God's Man in China:*

"In the first place, Hudson Taylor was ambitious without being proud. His ambition was nothing less than to evangelize all China, to preach Christ to all its people by

any and all means that come to hand. Significantly, God largely granted him his heart's desire. Men strongly differed with him and harshly criticized his methods. They thought the vast range of his vision almost arrogant. They were repelled by tenacity with which he pursued his objectives. They could not help having misgivings over the drive that took him to the forefront of all missionary work in his day. Such consuming ambition!

And yet, Taylor's sharpest critics again and again went out of their way to comment on his humility: 'How lowly he remained in his own eyes. God was able to take that beloved man and make him a prince among all the missionaries of the Victorian era.'

The second of Taylor's notable qualities was that he was unselfish in his concern for different fields of the world...The China Inland Mission was his great creation. To all its details he paid the closest attention. He loved organization and was a master at it. And yet, those who knew Taylor intimately found that his heart extended far beyond China and the CIM.

A friend commented: 'It was just as much a joy to him when men went to Africa, or to Japan...as it was when they went to China...It was the world that he wanted for Christ. No downgrading of other missions. No criticism of those whom he couldn't surpass...His call to his peers was that they trust one another more, and fear one another less.

Third Hudson Taylor was biblical without being bigoted. He was primarily a man of God – the God of the Scriptures. Because his life was filled with Bible study, prayer, vision, and faith, he was buoyant in spirit, venturesome, hopeful. Hudson Taylor's loyalty to Christ and His Word made him aggressive in his defense of faith...Taylor often used the illustration of the Russian who tossed out his children one by one to the pursuing hungry wolves, in order that he himself might escape their violence. 'Why appease the clamor of these critics,' he would thunder 'by tossing out vital truths of the faith? Don't have less faith in God than you have in man.' Here was a man of strong convictions...And yet, he was surprisingly free from bigotry.

Finally, Hudson Taylor was charismatic without being selfish. One of his greatest gifts was the ability to create strong ties of esteem and affection between himself and others. When he spoke, men listened. When he challenged them, they responded. When he went forward, they followed. Those who hardly knew him spoke of their sudden discovery – when in contact with him that he had a 'burning Christian heart...Some publicly doubted his ability to 'hold together his motley crew.' And yet, they lived to see him wield this crew into a strong missionary band. Some of his most unlikely co-workers became outstanding missionaries.

In this Hudson Taylor saw himself – God's 'exciter' – surrounded by men of far greater potential than his own. This greatly humbled him, and he resolved to try to bring out the potential he instinctively saw in his fellow workers. Charismatic, but without any trace of self-centeredness. No misusing of God's gracious gift to him. No empire building, no pyramiding of financial or personal power, no suppression of fellow Christians. Hudson Taylor sank all personal interests into a consuming desire to serve, no matter how humble or difficult the service...Here is the end of the matter: Hudson Taylor was Christlike."

J. Hudson Taylor was a man who dared to believe in the faithfulness of God no matter what the test. Because he acted on that belief, he became a man who saw revival.

John "Praying" Hyde
1865-1911

In 1888, a young man named John Hyde went to Bible college in Carthage, Illinois. He had been influenced to go through his oldest brother Edmond's testimony for Christ. Edmond Hyde was preparing for full-time Christian service. He served as, what was called in this Bible college, a "student volunteer" for the foreign field. During one summer vacation, Edmond had given up his break time to go to Montana to work among the "mountain" people. He contracted mountain fever, returned home, and died a few days later. Brokenhearted over his brother's death, John went to Bible college, vowing to do whatever God wanted with his life.

During his final year in college, a special meeting concerning foreign missions was held. As missionary John Herrick of India spoke, John became restless. After one service, he went to his roommate and said, *"Give me all the arguments for the foreign field."* His roommate replied, "You know as much about foreign missions as I do. Arguments are not what you need. What you need to do is go to your room, get on your knees, and stay there until it is settled with God." He decided to take this advice, and for the first time prayed all night long. The next day he told his friend, *"It's settled. I'm going to India."*

John Hyde immediately began to pray for others to go as foreign missionaries. He personally shared his burden for the lost in other nations with the 46 graduating men. Twenty-six of these men surrendered for missions by graduation time. One classmate named Lee, went to Korea, and in 36 years started 67 churches.

When John Hyde arrived in India, he found the people very unreceptive to the Gospel. For eight years he labored without any results. It seemed that no matter how hard he worked, and no matter how many people he witnessed to, nothing happened.

He finally decided to pray and fast until revival came. For 30 days he did not eat, and he spent each day on his face before God praying that He would open up the hearts of the people.

Some may have thought that results didn't come because John Hyde was very slow of speech. When a question or remark was directed to him, he seemed not to hear or he would take a long time to reply. Since he lacked in ability, he came to the place that he used prayer as his greatest weapon.

At one time, during these 30 days, he spent 36 continuous hours on his knees, begging God for His power. The Indians began to call him, "The man who never sleeps." Most of those who were later saved through his labors did not call him by his first name. They called him, "Praying Hyde." Not long after these 30 days, his prayers began to have their desired effect. Other Christians he knew became convicted about the great need for revival. These Christians would gather together to pray, and "Praying Hyde" asked those who were serious to sign a list of principles by which they would live:

"Are you praying for quickening in your own life, in the life of your fellow workers, and in the Church? Are you longing for greater power of the Holy Spirit in your own life and work, and are you convinced that you cannot go on without this power? Will you pray that you may not be ashamed of Jesus? Do you believe that prayer is the great means for securing this spiritual awakening? Will

you set apart one-half hour each day as soon after noon as possible to pray for this awakening, and are you willing to pray till the awakening comes?"

God began to answer his prayer. He felt impressed to pray that God would give him one soul saved each day for one year. He prayed that God would give him not only a soul saved, but that he would baptize at least one convert each day as well. This goal seemed impossible in India at the time; but after one year, he personally baptized more than 400 of his own converts! Even though he would win one or two souls each day, he had a great longing and passion for more lost souls to know Christ as Saviour.

The next year he prayed for two souls a day; and at the end of the year over 800 precious souls received Christ as Saviour and followed the Lord in believer's baptism through his personal soul winning.

What was his secret? His own words answers this question:

"When we keep near to Jesus, it is He who draws souls to Himself through us, but He must be lifted up in our lives; that is, we must be crucified with Him. It is self in some shape that comes between us and Him, so self must be dealt with as He was dealt with. Self must be crucified. Then indeed Christ is lifted up in our lives, and He cannot fail to attract souls to Himself. All this is the result of a close union and communion, that is fellowship with Him in His sufferings."

The next year he prayed for four souls a day. A friend recalled that if on any day he had not led four souls to Christ, there would be such a weight on his heart that it was positively painful; and he could not eat or sleep. He would pray and fast and beg God to show him what was the obstacle in him. God wonderfully blessed his humble heart, fervent prayers, and burning desire to see the Indians saved. "Praying" Hyde baptized over 1,600 of his own converts that year!

In my study of great men, I don't know of a man who had any greater burden or prayed more fervently for a foreign field as John Hyde did for India. In 1910, he was very sick and went to a doctor. The doctor told him, "This is one of the most unusual cases I've ever come across. Your heart has shifted out of its natural position on the left side and is now leaning toward the right side."

On February 17, 1912, at the age of 46, John Hyde died – literally of a broken heart. He had accomplished what his predecessor, William Carey, had said 100 years before his time: *"Expect great things from God, attempt great things for God."*

C.T. Studd

1860-1931

Of all these men who saw revival, probably the least known today is C.T. Studd. This great missionary experienced a great revival in the jungles of Africa.

C.T. Studd came from one of the richest families in England. He studied law at Cambridge University, and was the outstanding cricket player in England. He had everything a young person in England could desire except the throne. Yet, the will of God for this great athlete was to go to China, India, and finally to the heart of Africa. It was David Livingston who said, *"I'd rather be in the heart of Africa in the will of God, than on the throne of England, out of the will of God"*

C.T. Studd grew up in a Christian home, so he loved the Lord; however, he also loved cricket, the national sport in England. He was also very, very good. In 1881, he was chosen as what would be called today, "Cricketeer of the Year."

His cricket career at Cambridge was described as "one long blaze of cricketing glory." No one could stir the English as C.T. Studd could with his play. He was quite simply England's most exciting athlete. He said later that he never regretted his love for the game, but he did regret that he made an idol of it. What he did learn was self-denial, self-control, endurance, and a willingness to sacrifice for a cause. These traits were later evident and very useful in his missionary service.

His service for Christ was not a priority, and he said he always regretted this time in his life when Jesus Christ was not first. He was quick to warn others not to follow in his steps. In China he would later write to his younger brothers:

"I don't say, don't play games or cricket or so forth. By all means, play and enjoy them, giving thanks to Jesus for them. Only, take care that games don't become an idol to you as they did to me. What good will it do to anybody in the next world to have been the best player that ever has played? And then, think of the difference between that and winning people for Jesus."

While starring in cricket, his brother George, who was a devout Christian, became so ill he almost died. C.T. Studd began to view life as more than sports and popularity. D.L Moody was in Great Britain, and he felt a desire to hear him. God stirred Studd's heart, and he was never again the same person. Moody, the great evangelist, mentioned briefly the need for missionaries in China, and C.T. Studd heard God's call to go there. Believing his family would be thrilled to know of his decision, he announced to them his plans. Instead, he found most of them, especially his mother, very much against him "wasting his life" among the heathen people of China. Other relatives tried to discourage him, warning him that his decision to go to China was breaking his mother's heart.

"But, I knew God had given me His marching orders to go to China" he wrote, and he was determined to go – regardless of the cost. Before actually leaving for China, he had the joy of seeing his mother change her thinking, and she even began to encourage him in his work. This was the kind of person C.T. Studd was – a man of conviction whose loyalty to Jesus Christ was greater than to his family. He was a man who refused to allow God's will for his life to be sidetracked by difficult circumstances.

Six other classmates also became interested in China. Together they visited Hudson Taylor, Director of the China Inland Mission, who was in England at the time recruiting missionaries for China. These seven young men were accepted into the China Inland Missions and became known as the "Cambridge Seven" They were overwhelmed with invitations to speak about their decision to go to China. C.T. Studd spoke at Exeter Hall, London's largest indoor meeting place. He challenged the great number of young people gathered with the following words:

"I want to recommend you tonight to my Master. I have tried many ways of pleasure in my time; I have been running after the best Master – and thank God I have found Him..."

He closed with this challenge:

"There is enough power in this meeting to stir not only London and England, but the whole world."

The next morning, February 5, 1885, the Cambridge Seven left for China. While in China he turned 25 years old, the age his father's will said he was to receive his inheritance which amounted to 25,000 pounds – a great sum today, and simply a fortune over 100 years ago!

C.T. Studd never had to think much about finances, so he decided to give away all his inheritance and live by faith. He sent 5,000 pounds to D.L. Moody to start a work in Tirhout, North India, where C.T. Studd's father made his fortune. When Moody found out that he could not do this, he used the gift to start the Moody Bible Institute in Chicago. Studd also gave 5,000 pounds to George Mueller and his orphanages. He gave another 5,000 pounds to the Salvation Army, which at that time was a soul-winning organization.

C.T. Studd was engaged to Priscilla Stewart, who was also serving in China. He asked her if she thought it would be wise to keep a portion of the money for their future. She reminded him that the Lord impressed him to give it ALL away. He took the remaining money and gave it to other Christian organizations, and C.T. Studd lived by faith in China for nine years. When the two were married, they had about five dollars and a few belongings, but more importantly, God's hand of blessing was upon them.

He began his work, and it was in these early years of Christian service that he also began to see the power of God work in the lives of these people. One example was a man who remained after one of C.T. Studd's preaching services to talk. He told Studd, "I'm a murderer and an adulterer. I've broken all the laws again and again. I'm also a confirmed opium smoker. Your God cannot do anything to change me."

C.T. Studd told him of the love of Christ and the power of the Holy Spirit, and the man was saved. The first thing this new convert decided to do was go back and confess all of his evil deeds to those to whom he had done wrong. He wanted to tell them what Jesus did for him.

Crowds came to hear Studd. Afterwards the local leaders decided to punish him with 2,000 strokes with a bamboo cane. Nearly dead, his relatives took him to a hospital. Upon recovering, he was arrested and put into prison. He had a small open window and slits in the wall, so he would speak and give his testimony to the crowds who would gather to hear him.

C.T. Stood believed it was God's will to go to Northern India and start a work where D.L. Moody wanted to start a work – the very place where Studd's father became rich as a tea planter. He stayed there for six months, and a great number of people were saved. He then moved to Ootacamund, in South India, where he labored for six very fruitful years. However, his problems with asthma became so bad in that climate that he could only sleep between the hours of 2:00 am and 4:00 am.

After serving in China, C.T. Studd returned to England in 1906 to restore his health. He decided to spend the rest of his life winning souls there, and challenging the younger men to take his place on the mission field. One day in 1908, as he was walking down a street in Liverpool, England, a sign caught his attention. It read, "Cannibals want Christians." He couldn't help but laugh as he wondered what was so especially tasty about eating a Christian. Once inside the meeting place, he found a missionary from Africa pouring out his heart about the need for more missionaries there.

That missionary shared how big game hunters, explorers, traders, European officials, and scientists had endured all kinds of hardships to open up the country from a commercial and scientific standpoint, but Christians were not willing to go. He cried out, "Why doesn't someone go? Why doesn't someone hear and answer God's call? Why don't you go?"

The Lord dealt in C.T. Studd's heart, and he said, *"Lord, I'll go."* He went to the men who supported him in China and India. When he gave away all his money, these friends of his father began to help him. They asked him to go to his doctor for advice. He went to the doctor, already knowing what he would say. His doctor said, "Mr. Studd, you won't make it six months in that climate with your condition, much less a normal lifetime." He returned with his doctor's diagnosis and said, *"The doctor said I shouldn't go, but I believe it is the Lord's will."* The men met alone to discuss the matter, then they told him, "C.T., we loved your Dad, but we think you're making a mistake, and we can't help you."

He said he became very discouraged. He felt it was God's will to go to Africa, but how could he go without their support? For several weeks he stayed in this condition until one day he thought back to the time he had given away all his inheritance and had lived by faith. Suddenly he rejoiced, *"If God can take care of me all those years in China and India by faith, then God can take care of me in Africa."*

C.T. Studd got on a ship and left for Africa. Before he left, he wrote those men a letter and said, *"I will blaze the trail in Africa, though my body may only become a stepping stone, that younger men may follow."*

He finally arrived in the heart of Africa – the Belgian Congo, which today is known as the Democratic Republic of the Congo. He stayed there for 18 years; the doctors were wrong! At the age of 50, this man of God set out on his greatest missionary work and was to see revival far beyond any human expectation.

As far as evil and wickedness, what he found in Africa far surpassed what he saw in China and India. The practice of witchcraft, the vicious manner in which the tribes devoured each other, the inhumane customs, and the tribal secret societies, grieved his heart.

His converts went with him on his preaching trips in the remote jungle for as long as three months at a time. He trained about 20 men in preaching by this method, and established churches wherever he went.

C.T. Studd started many churches in areas where people walked for long distances to come to the services. One such place was Imbai, the church he started that he loved to visit the most. After preaching there and winning some converts, it wasn't long before people were coming from all over the surrounding areas. They built a building that would seat 1,500 people, which seemed out of place, considering the fact that there weren't 1,500 people within several miles of the church, and walking was the only means of transportation.

Revival came to this church, and soon the building was full. The natives walked hours, some all Saturday night, to come to church. C.T. Studd said that on Sunday he would wake up well before dawn because he could hear the Christians singing their Christian songs as they would be walking down the hills and through the jungle on their way to church. When the sun came up, the building was filled with eager faces waiting for the preaching to begin. From dawn to noon, the service would go on with singing, testifying and listening to Studd's long messages. After a short break to eat, all would return for the service which would often last until the sun went down. The members would return home burdened to win their friends and neighbors to Christ.

Missionary C.T. Studd had a Christlike spirit which included a sense of humor. At one time a fellow missionary was worried because of Studd's health. Studd also had a serious problem with his teeth. The friend told C.T. Studd, "You really need to go home and get your teeth properly fixed." His answer was always the same, that his suffering had been very small in comparison to Christ's. He said, *"If God wants me to have some new teeth, He can just as easily send me some here."*

Soon after a boat came up the river where he was staying. The new missionary it brought met one of the daughters of C.T. Studd with these words, "God has sent me to the heart of Africa, not only to preach the Gospel, but also to provide Mr. Studd with a set of teeth."

The Africans called Studd "Bwana," and you can imagine the shock and surprise of the congregation at Imbai when he appeared with his new white teeth. Of course, these natives had never seen false teeth. His new teeth were bothering him though, so during the prayer he took them out. Some of the congregation noticed after the prayer was finished, that his teeth were gone. "Who has stolen Bwana's teeth while we've all been praying?" they asked. They began to shout as some of the members began to run outside to get their spears.

He loved practical jokes, and with his new teeth, he had good opportunity. One day he put in the lower plate without pressing it into position. When some of the African workers came in, he set on a stool, took out a pair of pliers, and pulled out the eight new teeth with one pull. He said the expression on their faces was unforgettable.

There came a time in Imbai when a great number of the church members began to turn back from serving the Lord. Church attendance began to drop dramatically as some returned to idolatry, witchcraft, and even to taking part in the inhumane practices of the tribal secret societies. It became the attitude of some, that since they were now prepared for the next world, that it did not matter how much they lied, deceived, stole, sexually sinned, or followed customs against the teachings of the Bible.

This falling away was the biggest problem he ever had faced. He always believed the cure for this kind of thing was a baptism of the Holy Spirit and a great desire for revival. He knew it would only come when Christians were grieved, not only by the sins of those who had outwardly backslidden, but also grieved by their own sin first. The problem was compounded by other missionaries who had come. C.T. Studd refused to change from his strong belief that missionaries who worked there should live simple lives, sacrifice personal desires and comforts, and live by faith.

One night in a meeting with these missionaries, he was speaking from Hebrews 11 about the great heroes of the faith.

"What was the Spirit which caused these very human people to so triumph and die? The Holy Spirit of God...This is our need tonight. Will God give to us as He gave to them? Yes! Yes! Yes! What are the conditions? God gives all to those who give Him their all."

One by one the missionaries began to talk about surrendering 100% to Christ, and not to consider themselves and their needs important. They agreed to pray and work until revival came.

A great revival was started at that prayer meeting among these Christians, and it spread to the other Christians and finally to the lost. The church at Imbai became a church that sent workers everywhere preaching the Word. Some of these converts whom the Lord used greatly were the most unlikely.

One such convert of C.T. Studd was Zamu, a small, unimportant man in his village, who suffered from an ulcer on his leg that would not heal. He was often in trouble with other village officials as he traveled far and wide, preaching and winning souls.

Zamu knew about a large tribe nearly 200 miles south of his village. This tribe had been an enemy of his tribe for generations. After being warned by some of the Christians at Imbai not to go, he went to get advice from C.T. Studd. Knowing that Zamu, like himself, had a pioneering spirit to do what seemed to be impossible, the wise missionary told him, *"Go, and day by day God will give you strength. Don't be afraid. Preach the Gospel, and God will bless your work."*

Zamu and his wife began to walk. Painfully, he walked 80 miles through forest. They crossed the Ituri River and went another 100 miles. Upon reaching the Balumbi Tribe, he was received kindly by the people. However, they couldn't understand why this man would not participate in all the sinful things they did.

All was fine until he began to point out their sins. The angered people tried to starve Zamu and his wife. The Lord intervened and sent the brother of a local chief to help him. God blessed his willingness to suffer, and soon he had a number of converts.

C.T. Studd lost all track of Zamu, and after several years, he sent some workers to try to find him. Many of the Christians in Imbai thought he had probably been killed. Instead, they found his labors very fruitful. Zamu came back to Imbai and challenged the people to help him with laborers to evangelize the large Balumbi tribe. His faith stirred the hearts of about 50 members to go. They left, and revival spread throughout the Balumbi tribe.

By the grace of God, C.T. Studd saw over 200 churches started while he was in Africa. His influence went far beyond this great number of churches that were started, as his zeal and love for God was contagious.

He was a Christian who lived very simply. He had no savings, and lived in a bamboo hut. Walls made of dried mud were a far cry from the mansion in which he was reared. One of his daughters, who spent most of her life in England, had some bitterness against her father because he had given away his inheritance while in China. Near his death, she came to Africa to visit him. Like any father, he wanted to do what he could for his child. He looked around his little hut to see if he might find something of value to leave with her, but his search was in vain. Tears came as he turned to her and said, *"I'm sorry. I have nothing to give you. I've given everything to God."*

It wasn't long before his daughter repented and grew to admire the great faith, sacrifice, and love he had for God. Jim Elliot, the missionary who was martyred in Equador said, "He is no fool, who gives what he cannot keep, to gain what he cannot lose," Fifty years before those words were spoken, a missionary named C.T. Studd was such a man who had already put these words into practice. Our Saviour said it even better when He said in Matthew 6:20, *"But lay up for yourselves treasures in heaven, where neither moth nor rust doth corrupt, and where thieves do not break through nor steal:"*

Billy Sunday
1862-1935

Billy Sunday was born on November 19, 1862. After his father died as a soldier in the Civil War, his desolate mother decided to send six-year old Billy to the Soldier's Orphanage.

He grew up with a love for the game of baseball and was a very fast runner. Cap Anson of the Chicago White Stockings heard of him and decided to give him a tryout. Anson asked Sunday to race Fred Pfeffer, the fastest man in the National League. Barefooted, Sunday beat him by 15 feet in 100 yards. During his career, he stole 94 bases in 116 games and became the first player ever to be able to run the bases in 14 seconds. He became one of the most exciting players in the game.

One evening in 1887 after a few drinks at a saloon, Billy Sunday and five of his teammates sat on the curb of Van Buren Street in Chicago, when a group of Christian workers appeared, they listened to their music and testimonies. The song reminded him of the Gospel songs his mother sung. The workers invited him to the Pacific Garden Mission. As he listened to the preacher, the Lord convicted him of his lost condition. A lady named Mrs. Clark asked him to go forward and receive Christ as Saviour. He did, and that night Billy Sunday was saved.

He told his teammates that night, *"I'm going to Jesus Christ. We've come to a parting of the ways."* That night he couldn't sleep as he believed his teammates would make fun of his decision, but the next day, one by one, they came and congratulated him.

He began to help at the Pacific Garden Mission, and later began traveling with Evangelist J. Wilbur Chapman. When Chapman left his evangelistic campaigns to become a pastor, Billy Sunday didn't know what to do. He enjoyed giving his testimony, but he didn't know how to preach.

A telegram from Garner, Iowa, arrived asking him to come and hold an evangelistic meeting. He only had his testimony and eight sermons he borrowed from Dr. Chapman, so he wrote back and said he would come and hold an eight-day meeting. No one was more surprised than he was when 268 people were saved. He was already practicing something with which he would later challenge young Christian workers, *"It is not necessary to be in a big place to do big things."* He never intended on having large meetings in the biggest cities in the United States. He had not even planned to be an evangelist. He simply did his best when the opportunity came to preach.

Word spread that God was using him; and before long, he had so many invitations to hold meetings he couldn't accept them all. As he prepared more sermons, he increased the length of his meetings. Some meetings lasted nearly three months, and he would preach as often as four times a day. The Lord used Billy Sunday to preach to over 100,000,000 people, a remarkable feat considering he did not use a microphone. He would personally shake the hand of nearly all the estimated 1,000,000 converts in his meetings.

He worked tirelessly. His meetings were organized and managed with the greatest of care and detail. One professor of economics ranked his organization among the top five most successful businesses in the United States along with Standard Oil, U.S. Steel, National Cash Register, and one unnamed company. However, Billy Sunday knew that the real power came, not from his hard work and organization, but in the power of the Holy Spirit. It did not matter what the title of his message was, he always began his preaching by opening his Bible to Isaiah 61:1 which says, *"The Spirit of the LORD is upon me, because the LORD hath anointed me to preach good tidings unto the meek; he hath sent me to bind up the brokenhearted, to proclaim liberty to the captives, and the openings of the prison to them that are bound."*

He preached with all his might. He walked an average of one and one-half miles as he walked back and forth on a 30-foot platform during each sermon. Sunday didn't simply walk, he ran, slid, jumped, fell, and threw himself around the platform. He did not remain in one spot or one position for 30 seconds. When he was not pounding the pulpit, he would stand, one foot on the pulpit, and one foot on the top of the back of a chair. Then at the right moment, he would leap down onto the platform. Frequently, he would pick up the chair and bring down the chair, breaking it into many pieces in order to express his outrage at the liquor traffic.

As a young girl, my mother remembered hearing Billy Sunday preach. She said it was so long ago and she was so young that she doesn't remember anything he said, but she remembered that he threw a chair.

During the course of his most exciting sermons, Sunday peeled off first his coat, then his tie and collar, and finally he rolled up his sleeves. In this manner he would double up his fist in a boxer's stance, challenging the Devil to a fight.

Using only a sounding board, a crowd of 20,000 or more could hear him. Without whispering or talking, the crowd would keep their eyes fixed on Sunday.

Perhaps the outstanding quality of his preaching was its simplicity. Unlike the clergy of his day who tried to impress the people with their great vocabulary, intellect, and educational attainments, Billy Sunday would say,

"I want to preach so plainly that men could come from the factory and not have to bring a dictionary."

He was very plain and outspoken in his preaching against sin. To the intellectuals and educated who thought they were too smart for God, he would say:

"When the consensus of scholarship says one thing and the Bible says another, then the consensus of scholarship can go to Hell."

"Thousands of college graduates are going as fast as they can to Hell. If I had a million dollars, I'd give $999,999 to the church and $1 to education."

Some preachers were not preaching with power because they were afraid of offending people with the truth. He declared,

"Some ministers say, 'If you don't repent, you'll die and go to a place, the name of which I can't pronounce. I can! You'll go to Hell."

He preached hard against churches that were either filled with unsaved members or lost their compassion for the lost. Sunday cried,

"You Methodists can talk about infant baptism, and the Presbyterians can howl about perseverance, and half of your members will persevere in Hell; and the Baptists can howl about water, and half of your members are going where you can't get a drop."

No one in his day preached against sin like Billy Sunday. He didn't preach against it only because the Bible commanded it. He had a deep hatred for sin and was passionate in his fight against it. He would say,

"I'm against sin. I'll kick it as long as I have a foot, and I'll fight it as long as I've got a fist. I'll butt it as long as I've got a head. I'll bite it as long as I've got a tooth. And, when I'm old and fistless and footless and toothless, I'll gum it till I go home to Glory and it goes home to perdition."

In 1916, he went to Baltimore and built a tabernacle called the "Salvation Shed." It seated 15,000 people, and 5,000 more would stand during the services. On the last day, 24,000 people filled the building four times, so Billy Sunday preached to about 96,000 people during that one day. More than 23,000 people received Christ as Saviour. On the closing night, baseball star "Home Run" Baker and four other New York Yankees were saved.

In Kansas City, 40,000 people came in the rain to the opening service. In Pittsburgh, over 26,000 conversions were recorded. In Columbus, Ohio, 18,337 were saved. In Syracuse, New York, 22,299 received Christ. This happened nearly every place he went.

One of his most fruitful meetings was held in Philadelphia. Four months preceding the meeting, Billy Sunday asked the Christians to hold prayer meetings where they would confess their sins and pray for revival. Each night, about 5,000 prayer meetings were held with nearly 100,000 Christians praying for revival. The record showed that 41,724 people were saved during the meeting. With so many praying for revival, Sunday said, *"Anyone could come to a city and preach and have good results."* More than two million people attended the services at the tabernacle. Another one-million people attended meetings conducted by other staff members. No baseball series or political campaign stirred the hearts of the people like the campaign.

To give an idea of the size and organization of his meetings, in Boston he organized the following groups of workers:

8,000 choir members
2,000 ushers
200 door keepers
7,000 prayer meeting leaders
1,000 women to organize the city's businesswomen
700 secretaries
5,000 personal workers
1,000 women to help hold meetings in factories, hospitals and hotels.
500 women to care for children under four, as small children were not permitted in the tabernacle.

In the New York City campaign, it was estimated that over 50,000 workers were involved. He demanded that his staff work very hard; but, he got along with them, as well as the multitude of volunteer workers. He was friendly, easygoing, generous, and had a boyish sense of humor. He loved to play practical jokes. About his only fault in dealing with people was the fact that he easily lost his temper, but his anger never lasted for a long time.

Newspapers widely reported on his meetings. Some were very critical, and others praised his effect on the community. Sunday was even thankful for the criticism as he believed it only added to the crowds that attended. Some newspapers printed his sermons in full each day. Others drew cartoons mocking his work.

Newspapers would have quotes each morning in special-named columns like, "Sizzlers from Sunday's Sermons," or "Hot Shots from Billy," or "Nuggets." Quotes included some like these:

"Most of the forces of Hell are led by names on the church register."

"I'm sick and tired of hearing Jesus pictured as a sort who allowed himself to be a cupidor or a door mat. Jesus Christ was the bravest man who walked on the face of the Earth."

"I have more respect for the Devil than some preachers I have met: the Devil believes the Bible is the Word of God."

"Whiskey is all right in its place – but its place is in Hell."

"I have no doubt that there are men looking into my face tonight that have '1914' carved on their tombstones."

"They take a woman and put her on the stage with clothes enough to make a pair of leggings for a hummingbird. If I wanted to put what I thought about such shows in the newspapers, I would have to print my thoughts on asbestos."

His New York City campaign began on June 17, 1917, and lasted for ten weeks. The first night the crowd was so great that Dale Carnegie could not get in the tabernacle he helped to build. Sunday would always use sawdust to cover the floors, and the *New York Times* declared that converts responded...

"...until the aisles were packed and the lights were dimmed by the sawdust cloud thrown up from the trail by thousands of feet directed toward salvation."

On one day alone, more than 40,000 people were turned away because of a lack of space. He preached at the Plaza Hotel to 1,000 millionaires, and 221 of them were saved.

Over 100,000 people were saved in the New York City campaign, more than at any of his meetings. On the final night, he closed his meeting with a prayer and this farewell at the invitation:

"I hope New Yorkers, that we'll all go tramping together up the hill toward Zion where Gabriel blows the trumpet. Goodbye newspaper boys and girls. You've been great. Goodbye preachers! If I've said anything that hurt your feelings, well, you probably deserved it. Goodbye choir, you've been wonderful. Goodbye everybody. And now come and give me your hand for the last time. Do it now, for there won't be any tomorrow."

There was a rush to the platform, and 3,326 precious souls received Christ as Saviour that night. (A total of 7,238 were saved in the four services that day.) With tears in his eyes he said, *"I didn't want to go."* God had moved the hearts of so many, and New York had seen its greatest and perhaps last revival.

In the meetings he held, not only were souls saved, but homes were reunited. Thousands of these converts were young men whose mothers and fathers had prayed for them to be saved. Those who criticized Sunday's methods or messages would have a hard time convincing the parents of these young men who became clean-living Christians. Businessmen found out that a Billy Sunday revival meant that businesses would be run honestly, bars were closed, and cities benefited by the drop in crime.

One source of criticism were the prayers which Sunday delivered at the conclusion of his sermons. Moody, when praying from the platform, always said, "Let us pray" and bowed his head. Sunday scarcely changed his tone of voice, and when he began, *"Now Jesus You know...,"* or *"Well Jesus, isn't this a fine bunch here tonight?"* Audiences did not even realize that he had begun to pray.

Sunday's critics said that he was overly familiar with the Deity – a charge also leveled against Moody, who answered it by saying that he was not one-tenth as familiar with Him as he would like to be. Many clergymen not only disliked his tone of voice and his failure to use "thee" and "thou," but they also objected to his interrupting the reverential attitude of prayer to call attention to his own activities. *"We had a grand meeting last night. Lord, when this crowd came down from Dicksonville, or what was that place, Rody? Dickson City? Dickson City, Lord, that's right. It was a great crowd."*

"Oh say, Jesus, save that man down at Heron Lake that wrote that dirty black lie about me! You'll have a big job on Your hands to do it Lord, I'll tell You that before You begin, but go ahead. Better take along a pair of rubber gloves and a bottle of disinfectant, but if You can save him, Lord, I'd like to have you do it."

In the winter of 1918, he was in Washington D.C., and was asked to pray at the opening session of Congress. World War I had started, and the U.S. was a part of the war. The prayer made history, not only because it was the most unorthodox prayer ever prayed in the House of Representatives, but because it was interrupted by applause three times.

Billy Sunday faced much opposition, especially from the liquor business, which spared no expense to destroy him. The brewers even enlisted preachers to fight him. One opponent said, "It would be worth $1,000,000 a day to put Billy Sunday out of business."

Sunday hated the liquor business. America passed a law prohibiting the sale of alcoholic drink due primarily to the preaching of Billy Sunday. The vice president of an iron company said that he could pay $250,000 more in wages because Sunday's campaign had sobered up his employees, and they had become so much more productive. In West Virginia he preached from town to town, and he was credited with the 90,000 vote margin of victory in voting the state dry. He would say:

"I'm going to fight the liquor business till Hell freezes over, and then I'll put on ice skates and fight it some more."

One amazing fact was that many of those who fought him ended up coming over to the side Billy Sunday was on – the Lord's side. One such opponent was Al Saunders. He said, "I was tied up with the liquor business in Scranton, Pennsylvania. I said if Sunday came there I'd run him out of town."

Saunders came to Sunday's meeting to cause trouble, but was surprised when Sunday (evidently knowing of his plans) called out, *"Hey there! Old Scruff! You're going to Hell so fast they can't see you for the dust."*

The next night Saunders returned with some of his friends, most of them with bloated beer bellies. As Sunday entered from the side door, he had to pass them on the way to the platform. Seeing Saunders and his friends, he pointed to one beer-inflated belly and stated simply, *"It cost a lot to build."* He added, *"What do you have to show for it?"* Al Saunders said, "Nobody else heard him. That was just for us – a sermon in one sentence. It made me think."

74

That night Al Saunders hit the sawdust trail to the front and received Christ as Saviour. He left his old friends, and word began to spread. Al Saunders began to give his testimony. He felt guilty because, up until his conversion, he had done all he could to hurt Billy Sunday's campaign. He traveled all the way to Trenton, New Jersey to apologize, and found a way to sneak into Billy Sunday's house. Sunday was upset to see that someone circumvented his security. He had to be carefully protected. Al Saunders tells the rest of the story as follows:

"He (Billy Sunday) stormed out; 'Who are you and how did you get in here?"
"I said, 'I've come to apologize to you for the hard things I've said about you' and I told him what I said."
"He said, 'Let's tell it to the Lord. Kneel with me."
"We knelt and he placed his arm around me. Mind you, there was no audience, and no reason to be dramatic with me. I was nobody."
"He began to pray: 'Lord Jesus, this is Billy. You know why Al Saunders is here…' just like that!"
"When he was through he asked what he could give me for a remembrance. We thought of a photograph. So he got out his pen to autograph his picture. His tears fell down into the ink."
"Oh come!' he said, 'You don't want that!' and threw the smeared picture away. 'Rody' he called, 'Let me have your pen. I've spoiled the picture."

Billy Sunday was controversial, sensational and dramatic. But, he was something else; he was real. He truly loved people and walked with God. We might not all be able to be as sensational and dramatic as Billy Sunday, but we all can love people and God like Billy Sunday did.

J. Frank Norris
1877-1952

The life of Dr. J. Frank Norris provides a fascinating study of revival for fundamental independent Baptists today. All the men who have been studied thus far are missionaries and evangelists; however, J. Frank Norris' life is a story of revival in a local church. At one time, he actually pastored two churches! One, the First Baptist Church of Fort Worth, Texas, was America's largest Church. The other, Temple Baptist Church in Detroit, Michigan, became the second largest in the United States.

To understand the ministry of Dr. Norris requires a study of his early years in Texas. His godly mother, Mary Davis Norris, was the most influential person in his life. His father was a drunkard who spent most of the family's much needed income on liquor. He often would drink at a local saloon called, "The Blind Tiger." One Saturday night, his mother sent young Frank to the saloon with a note asking the bartender not to sell her husband any whiskey because they had no food. The bartender physically threw the boy out the door.

Frank walked the two miles back to his home and cried as he told his mother what had happened. She said, "Frank, go get the carriage." They went to town. She entered the saloon and pointed to the bartender and asked, "Frank, is this the man who laughed at you and cursed you?" All were silent. She noticed the note she had sent was crumpled up in a glass of beer. Without warning, she pulled out a horse whip she had brought and began to beat and chase that bartender across the saloon. The man finally fell to the floor and crawled out of the saloon. She began to smash the liquor bottles with the wooden end of the whip. J. Frank Norris got his hatred of sin and his courage from his brave mother.

One Christmas day, his mother decided to empty her husband's liquor bottles, so young Frank decided to help. When his father came home he said, "Frank, did you empty my liquor?" Frank told him he did. An already drunken Werner Norris was so angry that he beat his son with a whip until the boy was unconscious. The next morning when Frank woke up bloody and bruised, he found his sobered-up father weeping, and hugging him and crying, "Daddy didn't do it! Daddy didn't do it! Liquor did it!" Frank said his dad then prayed this prayer: "Oh God, liquor has wrecked my life and home. Take this boy and send him up and down this land to fight the curse that wrecked my life."

Despite the hardships caused by his father's drinking, Frank loved his dad and was proud of his courage. Local citizens had been frustrated because of the horse thieves in their area. Werner Norris volunteered to be the star witness against the horse thieves. Everyone talked of his bravery, and some bought him drinks as the local court organized the trial.

One day, two men appeared on horseback and began shooting their Colt .45's, striking Werner Norris. Frank was in the field when he heard the shots. He saw his father drop to the ground and began running toward the men on horseback with a small knife. One of the outlaws, John "Stokes" Shaw, fired three bullets into 15-year-old Frank. His father quickly recovered, but the boy was near death for some time. Gangrene set in, followed by inflammatory rheumatism. He became paralyzed, and for three years Frank couldn't move a joint without severe pain.

During these years, his mother used this recuperation time as an opportunity to instill in her child an unalterable ambition for great things. She read him stories of the great men of history. After three years of patient exercise, movement came back, and during his 18th year, J. Frank Norris could stand. He read much – the Bible being the book he read the most.

In 1895, "Cat" Smith, the pastor of the Hubbard City Baptist Church, befriended him. Frank emotionally and fearfully accepted the Bible as the complete and perfect Word of God. According to Cat Smith, the Bible must be accepted as a miraculous, absolute, infallible, inspired, and complete authority of God. They talked often and long about the things of God. Pastor Smith was the person who most influenced the kind of preacher J. Frank Norris would someday become – an independent, fundamental, Bible-believing, sin-fighting, Baptist preacher who also had a big heart for souls.

Encouraged to go to Bible college by Smith, at the age of 19, Norris enrolled at Baylor University, a Southern Baptist school. Some doubted this poor young man with the bad health could make it, but four years later he graduated valedictorian of his class. Going on to Louisville Seminary, he once again graduated valedictorian with the highest grade ever recorded at that institution.

Frank worked hard to master his subjects, the first being Bible. He had a consuming desire to know the Word of God. The second was history. Most great preachers have studied history quite extensively, but J. Frank Norris probably excelled above all others. Years later in his own Bible college, he would teach a class on world history completely by memory.

In 1906 he became the pastor of the McKinney Avenue Baptist Church in Dallas, Texas. This church began to grow, and then something happened that had a great impact on Norris' life. He had just finished his Sunday night message when he received a call that his mother was dying.

"When I walking in where she was sitting, propped up in a big armchair, her breath was short...I rushed up and said, 'Mother,' and she said, 'Frank, you got here!' I fell down at the side of her chair and she reached out her hand and found my head, and rested her hand upon it. Oh, I had felt the touch of that hand a thousand times! It felt familiar, it had touched my brow when I was wracked with pain, tossing with fever, it had been the best friend that I had ever had, now it was on my head for the last time, and I looked up at her and I said, 'Mother, do you see me?' And she said, 'My son, I can't see you, but I feel your face.' And she put her hand over my face and said, 'Yes, I have felt that face when you were a baby; I have felt it all through the years; but, Son, I am going home this morning. They have come for me. Do you hear the music?' And I said, 'No, I don't hear it.' And she said, 'Oh, I wish you could hear it. Never heard such music in the world.' And I said, 'Why is it, Mother, I don't hear it?' And she said, 'Oh, I hear it, they have come for me. I will have to go. Goodbye Son; preach the old Gospel. It's just like I taught you. Preach it until you come to Mother.'"

The funeral was simple, and his father came to the service drunk. J. Frank Norris spent that afternoon and evening alone praying; and although he never said what decision he made that day, it seems he returned a different person.

Upon returning to Dallas, he found himself growing weak physically. He developed a chronic cough and was plagued with insomnia. His weight fell to 128 pounds, even though he was about six feet tall. Despite this health issue, he kept on preaching, and his church grew in two years to over 1,000 members until the denominational leaders asked him to become editor of the *"Baptist Standard,"* a Southern Baptist paper.

Under his leadership, controversy and sensationalism soon characterized his paper. He began to attack race track gambling.

"I received a letter written in a very poor hand on cheap rag paper... It was signed by a broken-mother...who wrote me that her only son had gambled on races and lost. That he was caught and went the six-shooter route by his own hand. She wrote me urging, that as editor of the "Standard," I expose the great evil, so as to save other mother's boys. I went out to the race track and went under the grandstand. I saw 48 book markers... I had the whole thing photographed."

He began to expose this evil with this headline: "Racing at Dallas Fair – Gambling Hell." The powerful men who owned the race track began to attack Norris. The controversy was so great in Texas that the state legislature voted to outlaw gambling in Texas. Norris spoke at a crowded special session of the legislature. The racetrack owners brought 200 demonstrators to fill the gallery, and both sides gave their arguments. J. Frank Norris spoke last and was so effective in his message that he was allowed to preach on the evils of gambling until 1:50 a.m. He ended his message by reading the emotional letter of the bereaved mother and shouted, *"Shall we fail this godly mother?"*

This was his first big fight, and he learned that controversy often opens the doors to get his message across to the masses. He never forgot his lesson, nor did he hesitate to use any controversy available to him.

This fight had greatly increased the circulation of the *Baptist Standard*, but some in the denomination did not like it. Finally, in 1909, at the age of 33, J. Frank Norris left the paper and accepted a call to pastor the First Baptist Church of Forth Worth.

The vote for his call was 334 to 1. The members were excited that such a well-known man would pastor them. What they didn't seem to realize was what a controversial person he was. The one who voted against him later became one of his most loyal supporters. He explains his vote as follows:

"I am not opposed to J. Frank Norris, I am for him, but this church is in no condition for his type of ministry. If he comes, there will be allfiredest explosion ever witnessed in any church. We are at peace with the world, the flesh, the Devil, and with one another. And this fellow carries a broad axe and not a pearl handled penknife. I just want to warn you."

First Baptist Church with its 19 millionaires was known as the "Church of the Cattle Kings." When he accepted the call, he met with a group of men. They told him what a wonderful church they had and how they would take such good care of his family financially. Norris told them:

"Gentlemen, if I will come to you, I don't know what will happen. All I know is we won't look like we do now when we get through with each other."

The Devil began to work on J. Frank Norris, and he quit preaching hard and just enjoyed everything. These wealthy leaders gave him a beautiful home, nice automobiles, and every year a three-month paid vacation. At church he told the best jokes and didn't make any one angry or get anyone under conviction. The members really liked him, but J. Frank Norris was dying inside.

He was so depressed that he decided he would quit the ministry and move to California. He told his wife, *"I'm going to quit the ministry."*

She replied, "I didn't know you ever began.""*Okay then, I'm going to quit before I begin,"* he answered.

He had received an invitation to preach a revival meeting in Owensboro, Kentucky, for a friend, so he thought, *"I'll go there and preach and then come back and resign."*

At the meeting the place was packed, but Norris had no heart to preach. By Thursday he decided to go home without telling anyone. He took his bag, hid it in the weeds by the railroad track, and planned to catch the 11:00 train later that night. He then walked to the tabernacle to preach what he believed would be his last sermon. He tells one of the most thrilling stories I've ever read.

"When I got to the tabernacle and started to preach, the pastor leaned over and whispered to me, 'Don't you see that man sitting back yonder?' I had already seen him. He said, 'That old fellow with the red bandanna handkerchief around his neck – he's the meanest man in all this country. It's the first time I've ever known him to go to church – he has half a dozen notches in his gun. (Meaning he had killed six people.) If you reach that man you can reach the whole county.' I can see him now as he sat rared back – he had on boots and spurs, and I learned afterwards bells on his spurs, and he looked at me and I looked at him, and we were mutual curiosity to each other. As I stood there tired and weak, and looked at him and I

thought – 'You poor old sinner, it's the last time I ever expect to preach and I'm gonna give you the best I've got!'

I said, 'If there's a man here who is a sinner lost and willing to come to the Father's house tonight, Come on! Come on! My friends, I can see that old sinner now as he got up and started down the aisle – he had that old red bandanna handkerchief in one hand and his cowboy hat in the other, and you could hear his bells on his spurs jingling as he came. He didn't stop to shake hands with me. He fell full length on his face. When the little Methodist wife sitting over there, she didn't know he was anywhere around, but when she saw him, she let out a shout that could be heard a quarter of mile, and she came running and fell by his side. In five minutes there were more than 50 men and women at the altar seeking Jesus Christ, and salvation came and the eleven o'clock train whistled and I went on and they were still being saved, and twelve o'clock came and folks were still being saved, one o'clock came and they were still shouting, and two o'clock came they were still there. When I got back home it was three o'clock, and when I walked in Brother White said, 'Fort Worth is trying to get you'...finally I got my feelings under control and I said, 'Wife, we have had the biggest meeting you ever saw – more than half a hundred sinners have been saved, and they're shouting all over this country, and the biggest part of it is, Wife, you have a new husband – he has been saved tonight, he is coming home and we are going to start life over again and lick the roar out of that crowd and build the biggest church in the world.' She said, 'I knew it would happen. I've been praying for three days and nights. I haven't slept a wink, and tonight I had the answer to my prayer. I have been praying that this thing might happen, and my joy is complete.' I said, 'Good Wife, I will be home Sunday.'"

Deliberately, he set out to stir up some controversy. From Owensboro he wired a large newspaper advertisement to the *Ft. Worth Record*, announcing his coming Sunday evening sermon: "IF JIM JEFFRIES, THE CHICAGO CUBS, AND THEODORE ROOSEVELT CAN'T COME BACK WHO CAN?"

That Sunday night the auditorium was inadequate to contain the crowd who had come as the announcement had caused much discussion and interest. He only briefly spoke about the title, and then began to talk to the listener about Heaven and Hell and the cross. He lost the dignity he had always displayed in this church and pleaded with the people to make a decision to be saved. At the close, he greeted 62 converts who made their way to the aisle to accept his invitation. It was not uncommon in those days for 100 or 200 people to be added to the membership of the church on a single Sunday night.

He kept advertising sensational sermon titles, and the crowds came. Mr. Harry Keeton, a long-time supporter of Norris, often told of his first time to hear Norris preach. Mr. Keeton was an enthusiastic supporter of Ft. Worth's baseball team. He noticed a large banner across the front of the First Baptist Church as he passed by a few days later. The sign read:

"WHY DALLAS BEAT FT. WORTH IN BASEBALL. Hear J. Frank Norris Sunday night at 7:30 p.m."

He came to hear Norris preach as he wanted to know the reason himself. Norris only spoke one sentence about the subject. *"Dallas beat Ft. Worth,"* he shouted, *"because Dallas was better prepared for the game. Boys, you had better get prepared for the game of life!"*

Along with revival taking place in the church came resentment; jealousy, and opposition from many of the long-time church members who disliked his controversial preaching as well as the great number of poor and common people he was reaching. He had many fights, but he called this the biggest fight of his life. He recalled later what happened:

"The first thing I knew I got a call from the Chairman of the Board of Trustees. He was in the wholesale grocery business, a very domineering type of man, and he had been one of my closest friends. He called me up as if I had been the janitor and talked to me with less respect than I would speak to the janitor. He said in curt words: 'I want you to come down here right away. I want to see you.'

I started to tell him to go where the fires didn't go out. Fortunately, I decided otherwise, and I went in. I knew then I had entered the ministry. I knew that I was in the supreme fight of my life.

When I went in he never asked me to sit down...He had his feet propped on his desk and just rared back...they could hear him all over the place as he began to tell me what a fool I was, and what a mistake they had made, and closed by saying, 'Norris when we called you, we thought you had some sense, but you're a d– fool, and this is to notify you that you're fired.'

I walked up close to him, and if the Lord ever helped a poor preacher, He helped me that noon. I was made over. There was something beyond human power and wisdom that shot through my soul. I looked him squarely in the eyes and wasn't afraid of him. I had already come to the point it mattered little what happened to me. All the sense of fear was gone.

I said, 'Mister, you have the mistake in the call. You are the one who is fired. And next Sunday, I am going to tell the world of your threats' and I did, and the fight was on, and it's been on ever since."

During the mass meeting of liquor dealers in Forth Worth, a large advertisement in the newspaper appeared with a list of prominent citizens who were to host the meeting. The first three names he knew, they were deacons in the church – men who had opposed him. He called a meeting of all the deacons on Sunday morning before church. He proceeded to read the newspaper ad and said that either they would resign as deacons, or in the approaching service, he would ask the church for their church expulsion from the church membership. When the three left the room, never to return, they left determined to destroy him. Most of the other wealthy members left the church with them.

Norris began to fight the devils of Ft. Worth including "Hell's Half Acre," a part of town where 700 prostitutes worked. A private investigator, Mr. George Chapman, was hired to find out more of these illegal activities. He soon brought detailed evidence of 80 houses of prostitution. When Norris began to name the owners of the houses, many were prominent citizens of Ft. Worth.

Norris personally confronted some of these owners. One cursed him and told him those women were worthless and only fit for that kind of work. Norris announced he was going to expose them in a Sunday night sermon. He said, *"I got up the next Sunday night and told the crowd what they said and proved it. One thing is dead certain, the old church is no longer a corpse. Standing room is at a premium. We turned away more than we could get in."*

Week after week he preached about "Hell's Half Acre." He advertised the messages with such titles as "The Ten Biggest Devils in Ft. Worth – Names Included." Louis Entzminger, who came about this time to organize his Sunday school, tells about the service:

"There must have been at least 10,000 people in and around the tabernacle that night. On the opposite side of the street there was a Methodist Church, and a Methodist preacher trying to conduct a service. But, part of Norris' audience was actually sitting on the steps of the Methodist church and leaning against the wall and filling all the vacant space between the church and the street.

He had advertised that he would give the record of the ten biggest devils in Ft. Worth, and had written registered letters inviting them to be present to answer any charges that he made and to defend themselves. They were all prominent men.

The newspaper would not publish his announcement, not even paid advertisement...Talk about crowds – only part of the vast multitude of thousands got on the block – the streets were filled all around.

The 10 men had held a conference and had agreed to ignore the meeting, and nine of them did; but one of them, the main one, came...Norris carried out his full announced plan on all 10 of them, calling the roll and giving the record. The man, the top of the 10, when Norris gave record...went to the platform and Norris stood there quietly while (people) began to yell, 'Put him out!'

Norris beckoned to the crowd and obtained order and said, 'I invited this man to be here, He is my guest, and I want to give a respectful hearing...' Then the man proceeded, and when he had finished his barraging,

Norris stepped forward and quietly pointed his long finger in his face and said, 'Now you have had your say and I want to ask you some questions.' It is not necessary to go to all the questions, but I remember one of these very distinctly. It pertained to the ownership of the morning paper. The issue was whether the breweries owned it in whole or in part. Norris was fighting the liquor interests tooth and nail, and he wrung from this man the confirmation that breweries owned no small part of the stock. When this man made that confession, the crowd arose and roared, and this man walked away, head down, and ended the most dramatic hour I have ever witnessed in a public meeting."

The prohibition fight continued, and more threats were made against his life. Entzminger said,

"In the midst of the hottest prohibition fight any city ever had, a group of the outstanding men of Ft. Worth, held a meeting at which they voted unanimously to run Norris out of town. They notified him.

The first I knew about it was late one afternoon. I saw hand bills passed out as I passed along the streets...'J.FRANK NORRIS SPEAKS TONIGHT AT THE CORNER OF 15TH & MAIN AT 7 O'CLOCK.'

In that handbill the threat of these men was quoted, and he was speaking there directly in the face of the order for him never to do so anymore...The streets were packed and jammed; half the city was there, and in great confusion. There were three saloons, if not four; one on each corner at this particular place.

He stood in a Ford roadster to speak. There certainly was a mob spirit there. It developed soon that Norris had several thousand very warm rooters and supporters

present. It could have developed into a very serious situation. Norris led that excited mob singing, 'The Sweet By and By.' It quieted the whole crowd and they listened attentively.

During this same prohibition fight, a friend of Norris' came walking up to the church one day just as he and I started out to go some place. The friend's face was almost white as a sheet, and he was trembling with great excitement, saying, 'Dr. Norris, let me beg you not to go down the street, you stay right here' – I will not quote the man's name. He was one of the leading real estate men of Ft. Worth...' He says that the first time he lays his eyes on you he is going to shoot your heart out, and he is right down there at the corner of 6th and Main,' and he said, I beg you not to go that way.'

Norris looked at me and said, 'Come on Entz' – brushed by the man making some nonchalant response and off we went, and to my surprise and amazement, and I might add almost to my consternation, he proceeded forthwith to 6th and Main Streets.

Between 5th and 6th on Main Street was the largest bank in the city. In front of this bank was an old time hitching rack. Standing there leaning upon that was this real estate man who was going to kill Norris on first sight, talking to another man. Norris and I arm and arm, turned up the street directly to the place where these men were standing talking...All my past life came up before me as I thought of every mean thing I had done and what my wife would do without me. I did not want to be buried in Ft. Worth, or be shipped back to Florida where most of my relatives were at that time; I wondered about my insurance... We walked to the entrance of the bank within ten feet of the place where this man who was going to kill Norris on first sight was standing talking. As we walked up to the bank, Norris turned his back to the entrance where this man was standing, picked up a magazine off the display stand; we stood there just a moment, but there was no effort on the part of this man who was going to kill Norris on first sight to make any movement in that direction.

To my amazement and very great delight, he and the man to whom he was talking while we paused in ten feet of them, turned away and went angling across the street to the other side and off down the street somewhere… Norris looked at me with what seemed to me then as disdain and said, 'Entz, that's the only way to handle this crowd. If they had the least idea you are afraid of them, they would kill you.' And I am sure now he was right. I have been in all kinds of experiences with this man, and I say beyond all question he fears no one but God."

These weekly messages on Sunday night divided the city. He was to some a saint and noble crusader, and a devil and vile power-obsessed-preacher to others. Threats were made, and an attempt on his life was made as two bullets were fired through his study while he was preparing a message. He would always tell his crowd of the threats and attacks from those who fought him.

He announced a 90-day revival meeting during that summer of 1911. A vote was coming to outlaw liquor in Texas. He set up a giant tent, and the crowds came every night. The liquor interests got together and persuaded the mayor to tear down his tent. The malicious destruction of the tent dedicated to the preaching of the Gospel only increased the appeal of Norris. He continued to preach outside each night with no shelter, but the crowds increased. He attacked the mayor who had connived with the liquor interests to get rid of him.

J. Frank Norris found there was a large amount of city revenue, $400,000 to be exact, that could not be accounted for. He preached so much about this, and the crowds were so loud that the mayor couldn't ignore it. The Mayor announced he would speak at the City Hall auditorium, and the audience would be limited to "no boys under 21, and no women." Much preparation went into this meeting. Three thousand men packed the auditorium, and Mayor Bill Davis spoke for two hours and climaxed his meeting violently shouting, "If there are 50 red-blooded men in this town, a preacher will be hanging from the lamp post before daylight."

A few days on the evening of January 11, 1912, a fire was reported in the auditorium of the first Baptist Church. The building was partially destroyed by fire. A month later on February 4, at 2:30 a.m., the building was set afire again, and this time it burnt to the ground. A few blocks away, on the same night, a second fire was discovered at Norris' own home. This fire was put out, and most of the house was saved.

The mayor persuaded the district attorney, who was his friend, to file charges against Norris, saying he set the fires. The mayor began to pay witnesses to lie and to testify against Norris at the trial. A month later, their home was burned to the ground, and Norris was also accused of setting this fire. He asked for a quick trial. Thirteen attorneys volunteered and served him including O.S. Lammar and D.W. Odell, two senators.

In spite of the agony of going to trial, the church experienced more growth; and many were saved. The trial was then moved to Austin. Under oath, the final and key witness for the prosecution, a driver of a wagon, said he saw Norris at 2:00 a.m. outside under the street light, and that Norris had entered the church and that fire broke out a few minutes later.

Under cross-examination he was asked how he could see Norris. The witness said the street light was so bright, he could clearly identify Norris. When the attorney revealed the city records that the street lights were not on that night because the moon was shining brightly, the man confessed that he was lying. When asked who told him to lie, he pointed to the district attorney. Norris was acquitted of all charges, and his church rejoiced.

However, this battle took a toll on him, and he spoke of the difficulty and importance of forgiving his enemies:

"I learned then, and for all times, to win battles, I could not carry any bitterness of soul. Whether I wanted or not, I must forgive all men. I soon learned that I could not preach with any degree of power, have any liberty in the ministry, and unction in my message, if I went into the pulpit with any unforgiving sin in my soul against any mortal man. This was hard to do. It was a cross of crosses...I didn't want to forgive, and it broke my heart, it humbled my pride, it forced me into the darkness of Gethsemane to forgive my enemies. I won the victory through a special grace, and I had the assurance that if I surrendered all, that the God of all the Earth...would change my darkness into light."

He turned his effort into building a Sunday school:

"While we were having tremendous crowds, I fully realized that one thing was needed to teach and enlist the crowds. I did not know how to do that, and nobody knew that I did not know how to build a Sunday school..."

Louis Entzminger had come to work in his church a short time before this, and had a tremendous ability to organize a Sunday school. The Sunday school provided stability to the church as the spiritually grounded members became personally involved in teaching the Word of God.

The church built a new auditorium, but controversy stayed. One local newspaper hated him so much that they consistently followed their policy of refusing to print his name – not even in association with a funeral or wedding. He advertised each week with handbills that were spread around the city.

One Monday morning, a large canvass banner hung on the front of the church auditorium with the title of the next Sunday's message, "Next Sunday Night: SHOULD A PROMINENT FT. WORTH BANKER BUY HIGH PRICED SILK HOSE FOR ANOTHER MAN'S WIFE?" When the next Sunday night came, Norris made this announcement:

"Ladies and gentlemen, instead of one banker being guilty of buying a silk hose for another man's wife, three have made confessions, and the guilty banker in question has thrown himself on my hands, and has asked for the sake of his family, that I withhold his name. I cannot and I will not lift my hand against a man that I believe is sincerely penitent, and this matter is a closed incident."

J. Frank Norris preached hard against the Roman Catholic church, especially in light of the fact that the Knights of Columbus and the whiskey dealers were often in business together. He preached hard against liberalism in both the Southern Baptist and Northern Baptist Conventions. Many preachers followed his example of taking their church out of these denominations and became independent Baptist. This was probably J. Frank Norris' greatest and most long-lasting accomplishment.

There would not be anywhere near the large number of independent Baptist churches in the United States and around the world without him. Space does not permit the details, but practically every independent Baptist group has been influenced in some way by Norris' conviction of being an independent Baptist.

In 1921 Norris began preaching against evolution being taught in Baylor University, his Alma Mater. Many Southern Baptist preachers took up for the evolutionist crowd and decided to get rid of Norris. They protected an institution instead of defending the Bible. Norris went to Waco, Texas, where Baylor is located, and rented the city auditorium for $75. He announced that he was going to *"hang the apes and the monkeys on the faculty of Baylor University."* This statement roused a great stir. When he arrived in Waco, the sheriff and chief of police told him to go back home and not speak because of the angry crowd meeting in the auditorium. Norris dismissed the idea, told them it was still a free country, and that he was going to preach.

He said, *"I arrived at the auditorium an hour ahead of time and every available space was taken, and it was impossible to get in through the main door. I had to go into a side entrance and never was there such cat calls, hooting, booing, and yelling. They were plainly, sympathetically, and bluntly told, 'You are running true to form and are giving the finest evidence that your ancestors were braying asses, screeching monkeys, and yelling hyenas.'"*

Norris spent over two hours calling the names and giving the records of the evolutionists; and at the close of his speech, the audience was in "profound silence." Their hearts were moved, and when the question was put to them whether they believed the Bible or evolution, the entire audience leaped to its feet as one man. This two hour and ten-minute address was published, and it was the end of evolution in Baylor University.

In 1926 the mayor of Ft. Worth, F.C. Meacham, took $162,000 of taxpayers' money and gave it to the Ignacius Academy, a Roman Catholic school. (This mayor was a wicked man and hated Norris and the church, and he did all he could as mayor to make life miserable for both.) Norris printed 62,000 copies of his own newspaper, *The Searchlight,* denouncing this expenditure and sent his members to distribute the papers around the city. Norris also charged and proved that the mayor had paid $12,500 to a girl to keep quiet about an illegitimate child.

Meacham owned the large Meacham Department Store, and he responded by firing every employee who was a member or sympathizer of First Baptist Church. On Sunday night, Norris had each of those who had lost his job tell his story. The place was packed out as always, and he said,

"...Mr. Meacham's record is well known up here in Judge Bruce Young's court. A few years ago – it is a matter of record that F.C. Meacham had to pay one of his employees – a young lady, $12,500 besides to settle it. The lawyers representing F.C. Meacham were McLean, Scott and Syres. My friends, I say to this great audience, it is a shame in the name of Ft. Worth that a man of this kind should be mayor for one minute's time. There is no dispute about it, it is a court record, but if he wasn't guilty, why did he pay it? He paid it. He isn't fit to be manager of a hog pen."

Norris told the crowd he would have more to say the next Sunday night. The mayor hired a man named D.E. Chipps to kill J. Frank Norris; and the next Saturday, this man called Norris on the phone. Norris later said of the call:

"It was fifteen of twenty minutes before the trouble. The first words that were spoken when I said, 'Hello, 'were: 'We are coming up there to settle with you.' I said, 'Who is this?' and the voice over the phone came back and said, 'It don't matter you_____.' I asked him his name. He told me'...Chipps.' I told him that surely he did not mean what he just said. But he answered back, 'Well, I'm coming up there.' I insisted that he not come. I didn't want any trouble with him. But again he threatened me and said he was coming up to my office, and declared that he would not stand it any longer..."

The church bookkeeper, C.H. Nott, was in the office with J. Frank Norris when Chipps burst in. He tells what happened:

"When Chipps approached Norris, he stated 'I have something to say and I mean it. If you make another statement about my friends, I am going to kill you."

Believing he was in imminent danger, J. Frank Norris pulled out a .45 and shot Chipps three times. He staggered a few feet forward and died. Norris called the police and ambulance and finally, his wife. When the Chief of Police arrived, he took Norris to the district attorney where he was booked on the charge of murder.

The quickness with which the charge of murder was brought against him was indicative of the deep resentment by the city officials. Those who hated him spared no expense to destroy him and his reputation.

The church rallied, and the church newsletter reported the next Sunday that there were "15,000 present in all services, with 103 additions." Two weeks later the church paper reported, "An exceeding high day with 20,000 reported at all services." Once again he was acquitted.

Many of the opponents of J. Frank Norris suffered terrible fates. Mayor Meacham was put out of the office, lost his fortune, and soon and afterward died. The district attorney who framed and forged the indictment in 1912, was the tool of the liquor crowd. While driving his Cadillac (which was full of liquor) over the Main Street viaduct, he and his lady companion had a head-on crash with a streetcar. Both were taken into eternity. Their blood, brains, and the broken bottles covered the pavement. A half of a broken quart bottle of liquor was picked up from the pavement near the wreck. It was filled with liquor and brains. It was carried to Norris, and he took the bottle and brains and the liquor to his pulpit and preached on the text, *"Thou art weighed in the balances, and art found wanting."*

One of Ft. Worth's richest citizens, who was the "expert witness" on handwriting in the framed testimony, walked out on the railroad track near his house. He laid down, and a long line of freight cars cut his body in half. Many other people who fought Norris met a terrible death soon after they tried to hurt him. Twenty-nine of them could be listed if space permitted.

J. Frank Norris was a soul winner. Often he would be at the doorsteps of a home, early in the morning, while it was still dark. At sunrise, he would knock on his first door of the day. Entzminger remembered their soul-winning experiences:

"One of the most unusual experiences we have ever had was the story he told on me about pulling people out of bed at night to win them to Christ. We were both young and strong at the time and went night and day. When he

prepared his sermons, I don't know. The biggest part of the time for nearly four years we were going night and day after people.....if all were written, it would fill many volumes – night and day, summer and winter, hot and cold, sunshine and rain, morning, noon and night we have gone from house to house seeking to win people to Jesus Christ...I know of no man who will work longer or harder in season and out of season and who will go forth and pay any kind of price to win men to Jesus Christ. I have already said I do not know when Norris prepares his sermons. He has gone with me six days in the week from morning till night and preached two or three great sermons on Sunday. I do not know when he prepared them. I have seen him go home with half a dozen magazines under his arm at 6 o'clock or 7 o'clock in the evening, and go by his home at 10 or 11 at night and find them scattered around all over the floor or piled up in the waste basket."

Norris once said, *"I would do anything to keep a man out of Hell."*

In 1934, at the age of 58, he became the pastor of the Temple Baptist Church in Detroit, Michigan. On alternate weekends, he would preach in Ft. Worth and Detroit (over 1,000 miles away) and pastor both churches. Temple Baptist Church grew rapidly. During the summer he would follow the example in Ft. Worth by having giant tent revivals in public places. From the Ford Motor Company, he secured a large five-pole exhibition tent that covered 45,000 square feet. Before the summer was over, the crowds swelled to over 8,000 people, and hundreds of converts became members of Temple Baptist. The church grew to become the second largest church in the United States, second only to his church in Ft. Worth.

Someone once said of J. Frank Norris: "When the Lord made Norris, He found that he had run out of the element of fear, so He made him without fear."

Dr. J. Frank Norris did have fear, but he feared only the Lord. In August of 1952, he went home to be with the Lord; but his influence remains with us still.

Jack Hyles
1926-2001

The last man we will study is Dr. Jack Hyles. Knowing Brother Hyles personally made it easier to write about him. I first met Dr. Hyles in Springfield, Missouri, in November of 1973. I determined that night to go to Hyles-Anderson College. Since that time, it was my privilege to know him, both as the man who had been my pastor, and also as a friend.

Like Dr. J. Frank Norris, our study of him should be especially beneficial since these two men are the only two we've studied who were pastors. There are many similarities in the life of J. Frank Norris and Dr. Jack Hyles. Both had fathers with drinking problems, both had mothers who became the most influential person in their lives, both were used by God to build great churches, and both stirred up much controversy.

There are also differences in some respects. Although both men were involved in plenty of controversy, J. Frank Norris liked it and even looked for it. Bro. Hyles did not like controversy. He got into a lot of it because he preached and did what he believed was right. He had both moral and physical courage. He had been shot at, and had physical attacks against him. Attempts were made to burn down his house (unsuccessfully) and his church (successfully). He was attacked by the media, the new evangelicals, the Catholics and others. He did not like to fight. Courage is not the absence of fear, but courage is when a person does what is right even when he is afraid. In other words, he did what was right knowing that it is going to cost him; but he didn't dwell on the cost so much that he compromised. Bro. Hyles often said, *"I'm willing to make enemies over my position, but not because of my disposition."* He desired to get along with people. One other great attribute was that he was a very compassionate person.

Like J. Frank Norris, Jack Hyles was a great motivator. But, by his own admission, J. Frank Norris was not a great organizer. On the other hand, Brother Hyles was very efficient and probably will have more lasting results. His work also included authoring 50 books and pamphlets.

The ministry of First Baptist Church of Hammond, Indiana, was more complex than Dr. Norris' church; and the church continually started new ministries. That was a result of Bro. Hyles' meticulous planning and organization. His methods of reaching people have been widely copied, and the annual Pastors' School attracted about 7,000 delegates (mostly pastors) each year. Simply put, Bro. Hyles was a man who saw revival.

On September 25, two months and nine days after that fateful day in 1926, when Chipps was killed in the office of J. Frank Norris, a boy named Jack Hyles was born not far from Ft. Worth. As J. Frank Norris awaited his court trial to begin the following January, Jack Hyles would soon experience trials of his own.

The Hyles' family was very poor, so they moved to Dallas to find work. The Hyles' first child, Lorene, died at age 7. The second, Hazel, also died at age 7. His father was unsaved, but attended church when he was first married. By the time Jack Hyles was born (their fourth child), he had stopped attending church and began to drink heavily. Athey Hyles was a very big and strong man. He worked as a farmer, and once owned a small grocery store that went bankrupt during the Depression. He also worked in a cotton field, a dairy, bought and sold cattle, and he laid oak floor.

His mother helped pay the bills by cleaning a church building for $2 a week. They moved 18 times in his first 18 years – but never far from the same church. None of these old run-down houses had indoor plumbing, and one of his chores was carrying water for his family.

Young "Jackie-boy" Hyles loved baseball and played with a ball that was made by stuffing old socks and wrapping them in paper. His first bike was a broken one someone had thrown away. His mother sacrificed much for him, and this brought a determination that one day he would take good care of her, an opportunity God allowed him to fulfill. They were often hungry. He recalls,

"I shall never forget one night. My dad didn't come home. He was out drunk, We had nothing to eat, so Momma came to me and said, 'Son, let's go to bed early tonight.' I thought, 'Well...okay.' Then I heard Momma crying. I didn't know why, but now I realize it was because there was nothing to eat, and no wood to put in the stove. About four o'clock in the morning I heard mother open the door. Daddy came stumbling in, and the car was torn up; he was broke and bloody. There wasn't anything worth living for, it seemed."

His mother would cut pictures of beer bottles out of the newspaper and show them to young Jack and say, "No! No! No! No! No!" She made him repeat, "No! No! No! No! No!" and then stomp on the picture. He grew up with a deep hatred of sin, especially drinking. He was a very nervous child, often wondering if his dad would leave his mother. One day his father surprised him by saying he would join them at church that Sunday night.

Hoping his dad would get saved, he went to the pastor and asked him to preach on the Second Coming. That Sunday night, the church had a special program without any preaching. His dad didn't hear the Gospel. This event caused Bro. Hyles to later vow as a young pastor that he would always have preaching at his church services.

Cindy, his daughter, wrote that her dad's lonely teenage years began when his mother told him his father was leaving. He was gone from home a lot over the years, but this time it was for good. Jack asked his mom that if his dad would stop drinking if he could stay. She said, "Yes." On his knees, Jack then begged his dad, *"Wouldn't you rather have me than a bottle of beer?"* His dad said nothing. He walked away and never returned. From that time, Jack only saw his dad when he would occasionally ask his son to meet him on a certain corner for ten minutes or so.

As a teenager, Jack Hyles was tested in his Christian life. (He was saved at age 11.) He kept his promise to his mother and the Lord to never drink, smoke, or curse. As mentioned earlier, he loved baseball and became very good at pitching. During the summer that he graduated from high school, he pitched softball for the Dallas Railway and Terminal Company. The team won the city championship. The state finals were being held in Dallas that year. He pitched one no-hit game, and struck out at least ten batters in each game he pitched. To complicate matters, he was the only pitcher on the team, and for several days he knew the championship would be played on Sunday evening at 7:00. As Sunday drew closer, he battled with his conscience whether he would play on Sunday. The coach, a member in the church, rationalized, "Jack, you have a decision to make." Jack made the decision and said, *"I'm going to church."* His sister said, "It won't hurt to miss church just one time. Bro. Hyles responded, *"It won't hurt someone else, but it will hurt me."* When he arrived at church, the coach had the team dressed in their uniforms, sitting across the street from the church. They met him as he walked up the church steps. The coach argued, "If you played shortstop, it wouldn't hurt us, but you are our only pitcher." With no encouragement from the adult leadership, he stood alone, refusing to pitch the game.

Other experiences similar to this in his early years taught him to stand alone. While he was working at the Dallas Railway Terminal that summer, a Christian co-worker startled him when he said, "God told me you ought to be a preacher." For the first time in his life, Jack began to think about it. Soon after he was drafted into the army, and a few days before leaving, he attended a watch night service. On that night, December 31, 1944, he surrendered to preach. When he told the pastor of his decision, the pastor said, "Are you sure?" His pastor didn't think he could ever preach.

After he was called to preach, his dad called him and asked to meet him in downtown Dallas. There, young Jack said, *"Dad, God has called me to be a preacher."* His dad got angry and cursed him. He pushed his son so hard against the wall that he was nearly unconscience. Athey Hyles walked halfway across the street and then walked back. He kicked his son in the side and said, "My son, a – preacher." Then he yelled out, "You want to be a – Preacher, son of a – preacher." Then he yelled out, "You want to be a – son of a – preacher? WHY DON'T YOU BUILD THE BIGGEST CHURCH IN THE WORLD?" His father's words were certainly prophetic.

After serving as a paratrooper, Hyles left the army in 1949, and enrolled in East Texas State College. His first church was the Marris Chapel Baptist Church in Bogota, Texas. There were 19 members, and the church grew to only 20 in one year. The church was a poor church. No one in the congregation even had an indoor restroom. Bro. Hyles said the only member with a telephone was nearly deaf.

One Sunday he preached for the Grange Hall Baptist Church in Marshall, Texas, as the church had no pastor. Two other men had candidated for the church, and Bro. Hyles wasn't interested in the church. He was only preaching because a friend was a member there. A vote was taken the next week. One of the men on the ballot received 17 votes, and the other one received 9. Bro. Hyles received 27 write-in votes! One lady, and the teenagers in the church, voted for Bro. Hyles. The deacons were furious. They called him on the phone and demanded that he come to the church immediately. They had just concluded the deacon's meeting, and it was after midnight.

"Young man," one man said, "You're not old enough to pastor this church. I own the largest store in town, and most of the members rent from me." Another threatened, "You will not walk into the pulpit next Sunday." Bro. Hyles replied, *"You come this Sunday morning, and you'll see both these feet behind the pulpit."*

Bro. Hyles didn't sleep that night, but drove the country roads of East Texas. Finally, he stopped to pray in a pine thicket, kneeling on a sand hill. That night he determined five principles by which he would live. He took out some scratch paper and wrote the following principles:

1) I will not allow anyone to meddle with my preaching.

2) I will not make money an issue in my ministry.

3) I will be a friend to my friends.

4) I will be loyal to principles, and not to institutions.

5) I will base every decision on right and wrong and not on its outcome.

Once, a member came to complain to him about his sermon. Bro. Hyles stopped him and said, *"When we construct a new building, you get one vote. When we approve a budget, you get one vote. When we call a new staff member, you get one vote. But, when I preach, you don't get a vote. That's between me and God."*

For 12 weeks they didn't pay Bro. Hyles. On several occasions, the deacons sat and made faces at him while he preached. One night, God gave him the verse in Jeremiah 1:8, *"Be not afraid of their faces:..."* He announced to the congregation on a Sunday evening, *"Look what I found in the Bible! God says, I'm not supposed to be afraid of their faces."* Then he pointed to the deacons and said, *"You, and you, and you have been making faces at me when I preached. God tells me not to be afraid of you."*

On January 1, 1950, his dad came to hear him preach. Here is Bro. Hyles' recollection:

"On December 31, 1949, I found my father in a tavern. I walked inside that tavern and said, 'Dad, you're going home with me this weekend. You're going to Marshall, Texas, with me today, and I'm going to preach to you tomorrow on New Year's Day.' I took my dad to my car, and onto Marshall, Texas. On New Year's Eve night we had a Watch Night service, a blessed time. I said to my father, 'Dad, are you having a good time?' He looked at me, smiled, and great big tears rolled down his whiskered cheeks as he said, 'Son, they don't have this much fun where I stay.' I took him outside the building and said, 'Dad, I'm so happy! I want you to be one of my deacons. I want you to get saved.' Dad began to cry, 'Son, I would

love to be one of your deacons.' 'Dad, would you receive Christ?' He didn't receive Christ that night. The next morning I preached to him. He actually dug his fingernails into the pew as he went and cried, but he didn't come. I closed the service and said, 'He'll come tonight! He'll come tonight!' "That afternoon we went out in the pasture near the little country church. I put my arm around his big shoulders and said, 'Daddy, I've always wanted you to be a Christian. I'm a preacher, a pastor; but Dad, you drink, you curse, you are separated from mother; our home is broken. Won't you receive Christ as your Saviour?' My dad put his arm on my shoulder, looked me in the eye and said, 'Son, I'm going to come to East Texas and buy a little fruit stand and grocery store and go in business down here. I'm going to hear you preach every Sunday. I'm going to receive Christ and let you baptize me."

Soon after this his father died. Bro. Hyles tells in a sermon entitled, "The Fullness of the Spirit," how God used his death:

"As a kid preacher, I got this truth. I read every book I could find on the Holy Spirit. I said, 'Dear God, I'm willing to go into fanaticism.' I did not do so, and do not think it necessary to do so, but I said, 'Dear God, if I find it in the Bible, I'll seek for it, whatever it is.' I used to stay awake at night in the pine thicket in east Texas. If you would have driven down Highway 43 at 2:00 and 3:00 in the morning, you would have hearkened a young preacher crying in the woods, 'Where is the Lord God of Elijah? Where is the Lord God of Elijah?' Oh, all night prayer meetings over and over again. One day, the telephone rang, and the operator said, 'Rev. Jack Hyles?' And I said, 'This is he.' She said, 'Long distance call from Dallas, Texas.' A voice, a male voice said, 'Rev. Hyles?' And I said, 'Yes,' He said, 'Your daddy just dropped dead with a heart attack.' I

buried my drunkard dad. After the graveside service, I went back to the cemetery. No one was there but me. I knelt on his grave. I put my face next to the marker. I prostrated myself on that little mound. In a little town called Italy, Texas, I said, 'Dear God, if I had the power of God, my dad wouldn't have been in a drunkard's grave. I'm not going to leave until something happens to me.' I did not see angel's wings. I did not speak in some other language. I did not see Gabriel face to face. But, I got off my face a different man. How long I stayed I do not know. I have no idea. But I would betray my Lord today if I did not say then and there for the first time, I knew I was filled with the Holy Spirit. And my dear Christian, you cannot account to a fellow like me apart from that. You can't! There's no way in the world. I'm not a ten-talented person. I'm not a gifted person. But, thanks be to God, you don't have to be if you're anointed with the Holy Spirit of God."

When his father died, he didn't leave his family anything, except a $700 funeral bill. However, revival broke out in the Grange Hall Baptist Church. Bro. Hyles describes it at follows:

"I went back to Grange Hall Baptist Church the next Sunday. That night I got to preach, and the flood tides of Heaven began to turn loose. I preached a simple message – I don't know what it was on. Maybe it was Elijah or something. When I got through preaching, I gave the invitation and three people came to Jesus. Three. That was three times as many as I had had the first six months! I was so happy. Folks were leaving the service and I was so happy! I was still standing at the altar rejoicing in the Lord that three people got saved. I was in ecstasy. All of a sudden, from behind me a great big 235 pound fellow hit me from the rear. He was draped all over me. 'Bro. Hyles, my 17 year old daughter wants to get

saved. Will you go talk to her?' I didn't walk down the aisle; I walked across the pews! I told her about Jesus, and she got converted. I went out on the porch and said, 'Hey, come on back in folks! Barbara got saved!' And the folks got out of their cars and came back in the church house, and we voted Barbara in. They came to shake her hand. We all waited then had the benediction. Boy, that was wonderful. I said, 'This is tremendous! Praise God!'

We dismissed the service, and I was at the altar rejoicing when all of a sudden the same fellow – wham! He hit me from the rear. 'Bro. Hyles, my other married daughter wants to get saved. Can you go and tell her?' I went back in the corner and told her about Jesus and got her saved. Then, went out on the front porch and said, 'Hey, come on back in!' And they came back in, voted her in, came by to shake her hand. We dismissed the service again. Oh, I rejoiced in God! "Then about the time the folks got in their cars, the same fellow hit me and said, 'Hey preacher! Her husband wants to get saved, too.' I went back and got my arm around him, got him converted. Then, went out on the porch and said, 'Come on back again.' The folks came back in, we voted him in, they came to shake his hand. Six saved!

Again I was standing at the altar after the dismissal prayer. The same fellow hit me again. He draped around me and said, 'Preacher, I think I will get saved myself before I go home!' We knelt at the altar in the old church, and I told somebody to go out and tell people to come on back in, that another had gotten converted.' It was 11:20 that night when we got through.

We went home, next door. The parsonage was a little old cheap place. Mrs Hyles and I got our Bible, we opened it up and I said, 'Honey, this is what I want every Sunday, don't you?' She said, 'Yes.' Two little old kids who didn't *know John 3:16 very good – we got on our knees, opened the Bible, put our hands on the blessed Word of God and said, 'Dear Lord, we are not going to have anything but this. We claim it.'"*

He then became pastor of the Southside Baptist Church in Henderson, Texas, and the church grew from 100 to 600 members in eight months! He finished college during this time.

One day he visited a small church of 44 members in Garland, Texas, the Miller Road Baptist Church. Through a series of events, he became pastor and the church grew. They had 618 on their first-year anniversary, 1,180 on their second-year anniversary, and 2,212 on their third year anniversary.

Bigger battles came, and he was kicked out of the Southern Baptist Convention for preaching for independent Baptists and for having independent Baptist preachers like Lester Roloff, John R. Rice, and Lee Roberson preach for him.

These men were not approved by the denomination. Some of the influential Baptist leaders took it upon themselves to advise the young preacher. They invited him to a meeting at a cafeteria in Dallas. The room was packed with a luncheon crowd when the preachers sat down to talk. "We might as well get to the point," one of them announced to Hyles. "If you run with John R. Rice, Lester Roloff, and all the other Independents, you'll lose your denomination opportunities." Two or three of the others tried to force him to stop. Finally he had enough.

"I'M NOT FOR SALE!" Brother Hyles thundered, as he pounded the table so hard food spilled on some of the preachers. His outbursts silenced the cafeteria as people

looked away from their noon meal. *"You can't buy Jack Hyles"* he told them as he walked out of the cafeteria. Soon he lost all his preaching engagements and most of his so-called friends.

"People we never dreamed would leave us, left us. Folks we never dreamed would break their friendship, broke their friendship. I mean the best friends I had, I thought, turned their backs on our church and upon me just like that. Preacher boys whom God had saved and called to preach under our ministry, and everything they knew had been taught from our pulpit, left us just in a moment." To make matters worse, a tornado nearly destroyed his church. *"I was sound asleep and dreaming. The telephone rang. One of the custodians said, 'Brother Jack, come to the church quickly.'*

"What in the name of common sense happened?'

'A tornado hit the educational building.' I rushed down to the church house in the midst of pouring down rain and hail, looked up and saw through the top of our educational building. The top story was blown off and was down against one of the other buildings. The water was going through, and you could swim in the bottom floor. I looked at my associate pastor and said, 'Brother Jim, this is it! Friends are gone, members are gone, deacons are mad, preacher boys have left – now the building down. This is it!'

The next morning I got up in the pulpit. What did I preach on? On Job: what else was there to preach on? I got down to where I was trying to show them that God gave Job the victory and he said, 'I knew that my Redeemer liveth.' Usually I would say, 'Boy, I KNOW that my Redeemer liveth,' but that morning I didn't know. I didn't know it, but I said it. 'I know God is going to bless us.'

Look here, and I read the Scripture, and you know what it said? It said when the Lord came down to tell Job that the victory had come, He came IN A WHIRLWIND! Oh! I said, 'Victory has come! The Lord came in a tornado and told us that victory is here, and defeat is over!' By the end of the service, the people shouted for joy, the choir rejoiced, and folks were saying, 'Praise the Lord!'"

It was at this church that Bro. Hyles began to see what could be done if there were many soul winners in the church, not just the preacher. It wasn't long before there were 300 soul winners in the church. His ability to enlist and train soul winners was later perfected in Hammond, and partly explains the phenomenal growth in both churches.

While in Texas, he preached many revival meetings. One week he was preaching in a small town that was known for having a lot of bootleggers (those engaged in the illegal liquor business). The first three nights there were no results, so he began to preach against beer and whiskey, and the bootleggers got angry. They would pass the church and shoot their guns in the air. The third night he decided to pray all night. At 4:00 in the morning, the Holy Spirit spoke to his heart, "Go and find the meanest bootlegger and witness to him."

Bro. Hyles woke up the pastor in the darkness and asked, *"Who is the meanest bootlegger in this county?"*

"Vane Ward is the meanest. He will shoot you if he's mad."

"Let's go witness to him," Bro. Hyles challenged the preacher.

"Not me!" The pastor responded. "He runs the whole county's bootlegging, and everyone is afraid of him, including me!"

"But you're going!" Bro. Hyles was emphatic.

"No, I'm not!" the preacher countered.

"Okay, I'm going to tell Vane Ward that you said he's the meanest man in town." Bro. Hyles said.

"Okay, I'll go!" The preacher didn't want that to happen! It was 6:00 a.m. when they arrived at his home, and he was outside cooking breakfast. Vane Ward was 6'4" tall. Bro. Hyles walked up to him and asked, *"Are you Vane Ward?"* "Yeah, I'm Vane Ward," he answered. *"I'm Jack Hyles, and I'm preaching at the revival."* "Get out of here, I don't have time for preachers." Vane Ward shouted. *"I have heard that you were the meanest man in town."* Bro. Hyles said. "Who said that?" Vane Ward demanded. The pastor with Brother Hyles was getting nervous, but Brother Hyles said, *"Never mind who said it. This whole town is going to Hell. You break up homes. The families don't have food to eat because of your wicked business, and Hell won't be too hot for you."*

He dropped his cooking utensils and stepped up close to Bro. Hyles' face and said in a threatening tone of voice, "What did you say?"

Bro. Hyles repeated what he said and continued, *"What you ought to do is get down on your knees and pray and confess your sins."*

Both the pastor and Bro. Hyles were shocked when Vane Ward dropped to his knees and said, "This man is right."

Bro. Hyles led him to the Lord while his bacon and eggs burned.

Bro. Hyles told him, *"You need to come to church and walk down the aisle tonight."*

That day word spread all around that Vane Ward had "got religion." All the bootleggers came to church, but sat in their cars and trucks to watch. The P.A. system was turned up so they could hear the simple sermon Brother Hyles preached entitled, "Will There Be Any Drunkards in Heaven?"

When the invitation began, Vane Ward got up out of his seat and walked down the aisle, and people in the cars began cheering, honking their horns. Eleven drunkards got out of their cars and got saved saying, "If it's good enough for Vane Ward, then it's good enough for me." Over 200 adults were saved in the following days of revival!

Bro. Hyles went back to Miller Road Baptists Church rejoicing. He stayed at that church for six years and eight months, and God blessed. There were 4,128 members when he left. On August 27, 1959, at the age of 32, Jack Hyles became the pastor of First Baptist Church, in Hammond, Indiana, a suburb of Chicago. Unlike Texas, where people were friendly, most people in the Chicago area seemed cold and unfriendly. It was a difficult adjustment in many ways.

The church was very formal. The choir sang the seven-fold "Amen." The first Sunday he was there, the congregation sang, "Amen" at the end of the hymns. He had never heard it sung, so while the congregation sang, "Amen," he began to make announcements. Embarrassed, he decided during the second song he would sing the, "Amen" like everyone else. The organist and pianist decided the new preacher wasn't used to the, "Amen," so at the end of the song, they quit playing. But, Brother Hyles, in his not on-key bass voice, sang his first solo! "Amen, Amen, Amen."

First Baptist Church was a very important social church. It wasn't long before some of the wealthy members who controlled the church began to oppose his preaching and the kind of people he was reaching. Their opposition was serious, as his house was set on fire, but it was discovered in time and put out. Then, on June 5, 1964, he received a call at 1:10 a.m. from the fire chief. "You'd better come downtown. The church is burning," he said. An arsonist had set fire to three of the buildings. The arsonist was later identified by a photograph taken at the scene of the fire. Amazingly, he came back to the burning church and was photographed serving coffee and donuts to the firemen who were risking their lives to fight the fire that he started! Church services were held the next day which was Sunday. After the service, Bro. Hyles went to the jail to visit the arsonist.

"Hello Friend," he said to the man, who was very surprised by this greeting. The arsonist asked, "Why would you call me friend?" Bro. Hyles began to tell the story of Jesus Christ and how He was a friend of sinners. Bro. Hyles said that even though he had burned down his church, God still loved him and wanted him to be saved. There in jail, the arsonist received Jesus Christ as Saviour.

The church became divided, and in one week, 400 members left. The church went from 700 to 400 in attendance. Most of the wealthy and influential left; but God did not leave. Instead, God sent revival to the church, and by 1972 it was listed as the World's Largest Sunday School. That same year, Hyles-Anderson was started. In 1973, the church averaged 7,837 in attendance, nearly 2,000 more than the previous year. When Dr. Hyles was awarded a plaque by *Christian Life Magazine* for having the largest and fastest growing Sunday school in the United States in 1973, he said, *"I'd rather have the World's greatest Christians in my Church than the world's largest Sunday school. The world's greatest Christians have made this the world's largest church."*

The church began to reach the Chicago area with many kinds of ministries. Its deaf ministry and ministry to the educable slow were the largest of any church. First Baptist had a ministry reaching young people in the public schools, a ministry for the blind, a Rescue Mission for the homeless, and a ministry to sailors. The different ministries are simply too numerous to list them all, but the philosophy of the church was to win souls at any time, in any way, and at any place possible. The church baptized over 8,000 converts a year and averaged about 20,000 each Sunday under Bro. Hyles' ministry. They had ministries to many different groups of people who didn't speak English. The Spanish Department alone averaged over 1,200 each week.

In 1966, on Dr. Hyles' 40th birthday, he stayed up late praying for his future and what God would do to make his life more effective. He had been invited to preach in 22 city-wide revivals. But, the Lord spoke to his heart about the need to challenge, and also teach pastors how to have soul-winning churches.

There were three things he did to accomplish this. First, he began to travel every Monday and Tuesday to a different church. The local pastor of the church would invite pastors from all over the area to come, and Bro. Hyles would preach. Much of the time he would preach with Dr. John. R. Rice, the editor of the *Sword of the Lord*. They covered the United States, speaking every Monday night, Tuesday morning, and Tuesday night. God used these meetings to stir pastors to pray for the power of God to reach their area for Christ.

Second, he invited preachers from all over the United States to come to Hammond, Indiana for a week called, "Pastors' School." From morning until late afternoon, the ministries of First Baptist Church, and practical aspects of the ministry were taught by Dr. Hyles and the church staff. Special programs were held at night. Thursday night was often the highlight of the week.

In 1976, the theme of the Pastors' School was "Don't Quit." On Thursday night, Missionary Bob Hughes of the Philippines, who was dying of cancer, got out of his hospital bed in Dallas, Texas, and flew to Chicago. He only spoke for a few minutes. It was that night that the Lord spoke to my heart and several others, about coming to the Philippines. Countless life-changing decisions through the years were made at Pastors' School.

The third thing Bro. Hyles decided to do was to start Hyles-Anderson College to train young people for full-time Christian work. In 1972, Hyles-Anderson College opened with nearly 300 students. The college grew and trained men for the Gospel ministry more than any other Bible college in the world.

During Bro. Hyles time at First Baptist Church, the church was the most influential church in the United States, not only because of its size, but it's influence on other fundamental churches.

It is hard to find a good soul-winning independent Baptist church in the United States that hasn't been influenced in some way by the First Baptist Church of Hammond. Bro. Hyles' books and pamphlets, which have sold over 15,000,000 copies, also had a profound effect on fundamental churches, not only in the United States, but around the world, including here in the Philippines.

Dr. Jack Hyles was like Hudson Taylor in one way. Although both men probably saw greater results than anyone in their field of the ministry, (Taylor as a missionary, and Bro. Hyles as a pastor), I believe Bro.

Hyles will be remembered more by what he stood against against and by what he was than by the results with which God blessed him. He was an idealist.

To understand Bro. Hyles, a person must understand what was important to him. The Dr. Hyles I knew was first a man who believed in friendship and loyalty. He often said, *"I'd rather be a friend, than have a friend."* He believed that you can never lose a friend because if a person who claims to be your friend turns away when trouble comes, then he wasn't your friend in the first place. If Bro. Hyles said he was your friend, you didn't have to worry about losing his friendship during hard times.

After going through a very difficult time when several wicked men tried to destroy his reputation, I heard Dr. Hyles say, *"I'm a very fortunate man."* I was surprised to hear him say this. He continued, *"I'm very fortunate because I've been able to find out who my friends really are."* He explained that people never find out who their real friends are until they're down, and that it's easier to be against someone than for someone.

He would do anything for a friend. *"A request from a friend is a royal command,"* he once said. Friendship and loyalty were synonymous to him, and his fierce loyalty to his members who went through hard times resulted in a church that reciprocated this same kind of loyalty.

Once, when Bro. Hyles was being attacked, a good friend of mine and Dr. Hyles', Dr. Jim Vineyard, said to me, "Bro. Rick, when Bro. Hyles gets in trouble you never have to worry about him and his church. There is no one I've ever known that has people that rally to them like Bro. Hyles." I observed that although Bro. Hyles did not like controversy, the First Baptist Church and Bro. Hyles were at their best when there were opposition and trials.

Dr. Hyles will be remembered as a fundamental, independent Baptist. He will be remembered for his position that each local church is autonomous, and for his strong stand on both personal and ecclesiastical separation. He believed that preaching was always the main course to be served in the service of the church. People did not influence what he preached, depending upon who they were or what they had. He strongly believed in the local church, and that there was no such thing as the invisible church, so they can give an invisible tithe.

He will be remembered for his conviction that the main work God gave to the churches is winning souls. Through the years, as many others who used to believe these same things began to soften and change their stand, Bro. Hyles simply did not change. He often stated that in order for a preacher not to change, he must purpose in his heart not to change because the natural thing to do is change as others do.

Modern educators and intellectuals, who seem to think they are smarter than God, never impressed Bro. Hyles. His schools were not accredited by the government. *"Why should Christians want to be accredited by the heathen who are against almost everything we are for?"* he argued. In a day when the intellectuals laughed at the Bible and laughed at the fundamentalists who believe in a literal interpretation of the Bible, Bro. Hyles laughed right back. He once said about evolution, *"The strongest arguments for evolution are the monkeys who teach it."*

Once on an airplane, he sat next to a man who introduced himself as a college professor at Bucknell University. As they talked, he asked this man, *"If you died today, do you know for sure that you would you go to Heaven?"*

The professor replied, "I don't believe that. I don't believe the Bible; it's not scholarly."

Bro. Hyles asked, *"Have you read all of the Bible?"* The professor proudly replied, "Of course!"

"What did you think about the book of Jerusalem?" Bro. Hyles asked.

"Well, it's a good book, but it's not true" the professor replied.

When Bro. Hyles educated him a little by informing him that there was no book of "Jerusalem" in the Bible, the professor admitted he had never read the Bible. Bro. Hyles was not one who was intimidated by people like this professor.

I think one of the best illustrations I can give to show that he was committed to his principles came one day when one of his heroes, Dr. G.B. Vick, stopped in Hammond, Indiana, while passing through the area. At that time, Dr. Vick's church, Temple Baptist Church, Detroit Michigan, (the same church Dr. J. Frank Norris pastored), was the second largest church in the United States. The First Baptist Church of Hammond was growing, but at that time was a smaller church. It so happened that on the same afternoon that Dr. Vick stopped, Bro. Hyles had promised one of his daughters that he would take her shopping and would spend the afternoon with her.

He told Dr. Vick, *"I'm sorry, I can't talk to you, as I have a very important appointment."*

Much later when they met again, Dr. Hyles asked Dr. Vick, *"Were you angry when I didn't spend time with you that day?"*

"Yes," Dr. Vick replied, "I was at the time. But when I found out later your very important appointment was keeping your promise to spend time with your daughter, I was so proud of you."

If the words "loyalty" and "friend" were two words he treasured much, the words "quit" and "compromise" were despised. In fact, when I was a student at Hyles-Anderson College, those words were taught not to be in the vocabulary of a real man of God.

To some who did not really know Dr. Hyles, they only saw him as a man who stood for right and built a great work of God. But for who those who know him saw him as a more than that. They saw him as a man of love and compassion. He was extremely generous and would help anyone who made a mistake to get back up and serve the Lord. In a day when many Christians seemed to be unforgiving toward those who made mistakes, and didn't want to give people a second chance, it is ironic that the man who preached the hardest against sin may have helped restore more Christians to Christian service than anyone.

He preached very hard to warn people, especially young people, from making mistakes that would ruin their lives. He preached hard, not because he enjoyed it, but because he saw the hurt that sin brings.

To close, let me testify that it was a privilege to personally know Dr. Jack Hyles. I'm excited that someday I'll be able to meet these other great men in Heaven: George Whitfield, Hudson Taylor, J. Frank Norris, and others. Knowing Bro. Hyles was a foretaste of what it will be like to meet the other great men someday.

Can We See Revival Today?

BY: ALLEN DOMELLE

The psalmist said in Psalm 85:6, *"Wilt thou not revive us again: that thy people may rejoice in thee?"* This was a prayer from the psalmist that God would send revival in the midst of their captivity. The psalmist lamented in Psalm 44:1 when he said, *"We have heard with our ears, O God, our fathers have told us, what work thou didst in their days, in the times of old."* He said that he heard how God did great works in years gone by, but he desired for God to do those works again in his lifetime. In other words, the psalmist lived in a day when it seemed as if revival would never happen again, but as the Scriptures have testified, and the pages of this book have shown, revival happened.

My life and ministry have been about revival for over two decades. I have read about many of the revivals in years gone by starting from my early teenage years. I remember the night when God called me to preach, the sermon was about Jonah preaching and the revival that resulted in a whole city's salvation. This sermon stirred my heart to surrender to full-time service. From that time, I have longed and worked to bring revival to my nation. I have heard the naysayers comment that we are past revival, but I refuse to believe that. As long as God is on the throne, and as long as the Word of God does not change, I believe God can still send revival if Christians will meet His conditions. If we cannot see revival, then lets close all the churches and go live it up, for what is the purpose of serving the LORD if we cannot see revival. However, I truly believe that the stories we read from the pages of this book can happen in our lifetime if we will perform the same actions that these men performed.

Years ago when I preached for Dr. Rick Martin in the Philippines, he handed me a book that he wrote in a plastic holder. This book was not bound, but rather simply typed out and copied off to give people who came through. Because the book was about revival, it peaked my interest. I read the pages of this book, and God ignited a fire in my heart to see revival like these men did. Several years went by, when one day I was going through my books, and I came across this book. I read the book again, and the Holy Spirit began to do a work in my heart one more time. I read how the LORD did a great work in the lives of these men, and my thought was that every Christian needed to read this book.

While reading the book, I noticed several themes from each man that seemed to lead to revival. I began to write each theme down, and before long I realized there was a common string that caused these men to see revival. Over the next few pages, let me show you my observations of why God sent revival to these men, and how you can see revival if you will do the same things.

1. Each man did not seek revival.

One of the things I noticed in each story was how each of these men did not initially seek revival. Instead, each man initially sought obedience to the Scriptures. They were more interested in doing God's commands than they were with speaking about revival. Yes, eventually these men sought for a revival in the areas they worked, but their initial action was to do what they were supposed to do.

I find many Christians today who say they want revival, but they don't want to do what it really takes to have a revival. Revival is not a possession one holds; rather, revival is the result of obedience to God's commands. Can we actually see revival in our day? The answer is an emphatic, "Yes!" The way we will see revival in our day is to start obeying God's Word. You need to stop looking for revival and start doing what God commands. If you will do what God commands, then you will find revival follows. These men saw revival because they obeyed what God commanded them to do.

2. Each man made Christ the focus of his ministry.

It is interesting that each man was not interested in how big his ministry became; rather, they were interested in keeping Christ as the focus of their ministry. These men did not make themselves the issue in the ministry, but they made Christ the central focus of their ministry. They were not concerned with their legacy, but they were concerned with making Christ the focus of all they did.

One of the reasons we don't see revival in our day is because of the selfishness and self-centered focus of so many men of God. I have watched many ministries that are filled with self-promotion. It's no wonder that we don't see revival in our day. You will never see revival when you are more interested in what man says than what God says. When Christ is lifted up, then we have a reason for the Holy Spirit of God to involve Himself in our ministries. We will never see revival until Christ becomes the focal point of all that we do. We will never see revival as long as man and his ministries are what we strive to build more than lifting up the name of Christ.

3. Each man had a hatred for sin.

One of the things that is very evident in the lives of each of these men is their hatred for sin. They didn't curtail their battle against sin for the sake of holding a crowd or the fierceness of the battle. In fact, their battle of sin is part of what caused the crowds to come. They didn't hold their finger to the wind to find out if it was popular to preach against sin; rather, they fought sin because of the reproach it brought to the name of Christ and the hurt it brought to the lives of individuals.

If we want revival in our day, then we are going to have to have a renewed hatred for sin. As long as we tolerate sin, God will not send revival. It is always a hatred of sin that caused God's people to turn to Him. When sin no longer shocks you, then you have a problem. You will never see revival until sin becomes as disgusting to you as it is to God.

4. Each man saw the importance of the Holy Spirit's power.

This may be one of the most important aspects of why these men saw revival. Each man yearned for God's Holy Spirit to fill them. They realized on their own they did not have the power to do what needed to be done. Each man was willing to pay any price to have the Holy Spirit empower them.

Let me ask you, what is the price tag you put on getting the Holy Spirit's power? Is there a stopping point where you will go no further to obtain the power of God? If there is, then you will not see revival. Revival will only happen when you are willing to do away with anything and everything just to have the power of God on your life. Every revival in history happened because of a man who was empowered by the Holy Spirit.

5. Each man aggressively went after the souls of men.

It is interesting that each man had a great hunger to see souls saved. It was not just a requirement they had to fulfill each week, but it was a longing in their soul to see people saved. There was no length these men would not go to see a soul saved. They were not embarrassed to talk about Christ, but they boldly proclaimed Christ to the lost world.

There is no purpose for revival if you don't aggressively go after the souls of men. Soul winning was not a gift to these men, but a great concern for the souls of people is what stirred them to aggressively go after the souls of men. If you want revival, then soul winning must become a daily part of your life. God will never send revival unless we become aggressive about reaching people for Christ.

6. Each man lived in a day when sin was prevalent.

I commonly hear that we are beyond revival because of the wickedness of our society. When reading about these men, you find they lived in wicked societies. Many of these men were hated to the degree that people wanted them dead. Yet, they were not afraid to fight sin. When they saw sin, they called it out. It may not have been popular, but they saw that sin was destroying people.

Revival will never come when we are afraid to stand against the sin of our day. We don't need to use politically correct wording to keep from being offensive, but we need people to call sin what it truly is, sin. Just because we live in a day when sin is prevalent does not mean that we can't see revival. In fact, the opposite is true. Because sin is so prevalent, we have a better chance of seeing revival if we will fight it.

7. Each man made much of their personal walk with God.

One of the main reasons these men saw revival is because they daily spent time with God, Who revived their soul. They were not too busy to spend time with God on a daily basis. Their walk with God was important to them.

As long as God is on the side shelf, we will never see revival. It amazes me how many Christians don't have a time they spend with God on a daily basis. Spending time with God in the Scriptures and prayer is what gives you the heartbeat of God. His Word will cleanse you from sin. Time in prayer will empower you to serve Him. Yes, we can have revival, but only when God's people make much of their personal walk with Him.

8. Each man believed God could do the miraculous in their life.

One of the things I love about these men is that they were not afraid to step out and put God to the test. These men saw the miraculous because they attempted the miraculous. These men were men of faith. They had a faith that God still had the power in their lifetime to perform the miraculous.

God will not send revival through your life if you won't attempt the miraculous. These men didn't put God in a small box, and neither should you. God does not have a power shortage that He can't do the miraculous through your life. The only way He can perform the miraculous is if you will attempt the miraculous. You need to see that God is not a little God, but He is the God Who still has the power to perform miracles and send revival in our day.

9. Each man was not concerned with man's opinion of him.

These men did not concern themselves with the populace, but they concerned themselves with what God wanted them to do. The acceptance of man was not their biggest priority, but the acceptance of God is what they sought. They never sought to become nationally known men, they only sought to let God do a work through their lives.

Revival will never come if you are concerned with what man thinks about you. Your greatest concern should be with what God thinks about you. Stop asking man what they think, and start asking God what He thinks. Stop looking for a national name, and look for God's power. You will never see revival as long as you are concerned with man's opinion of you.

Let me close by saying that I believe revival can happen in our day. Isaiah 44:3 says, *"For I will pour water upon him that is thirsty, and floods upon the dry ground: I will pour my spirit upon thy seed, and my blessing upon thine offspring:"*

Let me ask you, how thirsty are you for revival? We can see revival, but we must be willing to pay the price for it. We can see revival, but we must long and thirst for it to the point that we lose our appetite for everything else other than what God wants us to do. When we thirst to the degree that we don't want anything else but God, will do whatever it takes to see revival, will forsake any sin that may be keeping us from revival, will aggressively seek the souls of men, will attempt to do the miraculous and will seek God's power on our lives, then that is when God will allow us to see revival in our day.

Quotes from Men Who Saw Revival

"Expect great things from God; attempt great things for God." – William Carey

"A revival can be expected when Christians have a spirit of prayer for revival." – Charles Finney

"Sin will keep you from this book, or this book will keep you from sin." – D.L. Moody on the Bible

"I'd rather be in the heart of Africa in the will of God than on the throne of England out of the will of God." – David Livingston

"A revival is no more a miracle than a crop of wheat. In any community, revival can be secured from Heaven when heroic souls enter the conflict determined to win or die – or if need be, to win and die!" – Charles Finney

"Give me 100 men who hate nothing but sin; and love nothing but God, and I'll turn the world upside down." – John Wesley

"The world has yet to see what God will do with and for and through and in and by the man who is fully and wholly consecrated to Him." (D.L. Moody, upon hearing this challenge said, "I will try my utmost to be that man.")

"It is not the greatness of our troubles as the littleness of our spirit, which makes us complain." – Hudson Taylor

"We have heard of many people who trusted God too little, but have you ever heard of anyone who trusted Him too much?" – Hudson Taylor

"Take care of your life and the Lord will take care of your death." – George Whitefield

"God always gives His best to those who leave the choice with him." – Jim Elliot

"I am willing to make enemies because of my position, but not because of my disposition." – Jack Hyles

Revival is renewed conviction of sin and repentance, followed by an intense desire to live in obedience to God. It is giving up one's will to God in deep humility." – Charles Finney

"I would do anything to keep a man out of Hell." – J. Frank Norris

"It is the subject of his thoughts all the time, and makes him look and act as if he had a load on his mind. He thinks of it by day and dreams of it by night." – Charles Finney on a burden for souls and how to see revival among the lost.

"Some ministers say, 'If you don't repent you'll die and go to a place the name of which I can't pronounce.' I can! You'll go to Hell." – Billy Sunday

"I want to preach so plainly that men could come from the factory and not have to bring a dictionary." – Billy Sunday

"I have more respect for the Devil than for some preachers I have met; the Devil believes the Bible is the Word of God!" – Billy Sunday

"I'm against sin. I'll kick it as long as I've got a foot, and I'll fight it as long as I've got a fist. I'll butt it as long as I've got a head. I'll bite it as long as I've got a tooth. And,

when I'm old, and fistless, and footless and toothless, I'll gum it till I go to Glory and it goes to perdition." – Billy Sunday

"It is not necessary to be in a big place to do big things." – Billy Sunday

"If I had my life to live over, I would give all my time to children." – D.L. Moody

"Is there a Hell? If I didn't believe there was a Hell I would close my Bible; I would walk out that door. I would never preach another sermon, and I would make as much money as I could. But, I do believe, from the crown of my head to the sole of my feet, that there is a Hell." – Jack Hyles

"He is no fool who gives what he cannot keep, to gain what he cannot lose." – Jim Elliot

"I will blaze the trail in Africa, although my body may only become a stepping stone that younger men may follow." – C.T. Studd at age 60, going to Africa in bad health and with no support.

"The future is as bright as the promises of God" – Bob Hughes

OTHER PRODUCTS AVAILABLE FROM DOMELLE MINISTRIES

PREACHING CD ALBUMS

- Staying on Top Side
- Lighting Your Own Fire
- Caution, Hot Preaching Ahead
- Sermons for Struggling Christians
- Relationships with God and Man
- Sermons for Hurting Hearts
- Making a Difference
- Stepping Up
- Standing for Truth

BOOKS

- Blueprints for Life
- How to Study the World's Greatest Book
- The Battle for God's Word
- Nine Steps to Backsliding
- Spiritual Espresso Volumes 1 & 2
- Till Death Do Us Part

DAILY DEVOTIONAL AND ONLINE PAPER

- Sign up for daily devotionals at:
  oldpathsjournal.com

To order these products and more call:
903.746.9632
or visit
oldpathsjournal.com
domelleministries.com